Tarnished Haloes, Open Hearts

A Story of Finding and Giving Acceptance

Lynelle Sweat Mason

Lynelle Mason

2019

Published in the United States by Nurturing Faith Inc., Macon GA,
www.nurturingfaith.net.

Library of Congress Cataloging-in-Publication Data is available.

ISBN 978-1-938514-01-2

Every Child Should…

Enter life assured of acceptance.
Be spared the pangs of hunger.
Have a spot called home.
Receive medical help in time of need.
Be surrounded by caring adults.
Be free of race and status blinders.
Have room to dream and to grow.
Live in a world where breathing isn't a gasp.
Be free to discover a God whose love is unconditional.

Lynelle finding laughter amid a tough childhood

Contents

Chapter 1

Dear John's Letter

"There was a special chemistry between my brother and me
that would always transcend time."

It was Halloween 1935, and my interest as a four-year-old in goblins and ghosts grew by twenty notches.

"Mama," I asked, "Do goblins and ghosts really run wild on Halloween?"

Mama gave me her most mama look, saying, "I hear tell that devils dressed in red suits and armed with pitchforks have been seen by mean little kids on Halloween."

I was about to believe her until she began laughing.

"Aw, Mama," I said, "you're teasing. There aren't any ghosts, goblins, or devils in red suits. Are there?"

Before she could answer me there was a thunderous banging on the window of our living room. It sounded like rain pelting down on a tin roof.

"Mama," I asked, "what's that noise?"

Mama pretended she hadn't heard a thing. She rolled her big green eyes and asked, "What noise?"

"Th…at noise. It…ttt sounds like it came from the window."

"Hmm," said Mama, in a casual voice, "I don't know. Let's go see."

I grabbed hold of Mama's apron as she ambled over to the window.

"Oh, my!" I screamed, "That scarecrow is ugly. Mama, don't let him get me. Make him go away."

"Now that wouldn't be nice, would it? Besides, he can't help being ugly. Maybe he's friendly. Let's go outside and see what he wants."

"I'm *not* going out there," I said. As Mama headed toward our wrap-around porch, I began having second thoughts. "Mama!" I yelled. "Wait for me. I'm coming."

That horrible scarecrow gave my siblings and me a merry chase. Once he almost had me in his flaying arms.

Finally the scarecrow left, and soon my oldest brother John arrived. He seemed to know nothing about our scarecrow visitor. To heighten our excitement, he draped a quilt over the front porch swing and told us ghost stories.

I'm told by my eldest sister that my brother John, the oldest child of Cleo and Ward Sweat, was loved and wanted by his parents, had good health, exhibited socially acceptable behaviors with adults and peers, and was intellectually curious.

John was an obedient lad until it came to sneaking away to see motion picture shows—a "no-no." It seems according to my father that going to motion pictures was a work of Satan. John would take his spankings and still return the following Saturday to view the silver screen.

When he was twelve, John was baptized by his preacher-father. Whether that involved any repentance for his trips to the cinema I have no way of knowing.

My father, who died at the young age of thirty-one, saw but one movie in his lifetime—*The King of Kings*.

Mama must not have harbored such strong views against the silver screen. The highlights of my preteen Saturdays were going to the theater and being mesmerized by Roy Rogers and Gene Autry as good always triumphed over evil.

At age thirteen, due to the untimely death of our daddy, my older brother John became the surrogate father to seven children younger than himself. He took this responsibility seriously. He sold fudge on the streets of Waycross, Georgia, and attended P.T.A. meetings for all his brothers and sisters.

Shortly after Daddy's death, ensuing financial struggles forced us to move to our family farm. That's when it was decided John would move in with our paternal grandparents—who lived up in the Forks of the Hurricane community near Blackshear, Georgia—until he finished high school. His trips to our farm were sporadic.

Our farmhouse at Dixie Union, fifteen miles south of Waycross, was my safe haven—especially when John came to visit.

Upon graduating from Blackshear High School with honors in 1936, John acquired a clerk/typist job with a railroad firm in Atlanta. He attended classes provided by the University of Georgia. He lived at the local YMCA at a cost of $4.25 a week and managed to save enough money to take tap dancing lessons.

John had been in Atlanta for a few years when his memorable letter arrived. I met the postman at the front doorsteps.

"Mama," I said, "we have a letter from John."

Mama wiped the flour from her stout hands, took the letter, and seated herself at the kitchen table. I watched as her soft face grew somber. In the middle of reading the letter she called for my brother.

"Go, get Skeet," she said. "Tell him to come at once. I need him."

It wasn't long before my next-eldest brother came bounding into the kitchen asking, "What's up, Mama?"

Mama didn't say anything but instead handed him the letter. I watched as his face turned crimson.

Skeet paced the floor while exclaiming loudly, "He never was like the rest of us. Even as a kid, he wouldn't play any boy games."

He walked into the bedroom and flung the letter on the bed.

"Queer, or not, he'll still have to do his share. Who does he think he is? I tell you, Mama, I think he's trying to get out of helping you pay the bills."

Now Mama was crying, and my brother stormed out the back door. I sidled into the bedroom and when no one was looking, picked up the letter.

The letter started off with the usual stuff ranging from health, weather, and work. Then my eye caught the following sentence: "Mama, from now on you must think of me as your eldest daughter."

I read it again and again trying to make sense out of what my brother John had written. Daughter? What did he mean? Why was Mama crying? Why was my brother Skeet so angry?

Big brother John

I was overwhelmed by a maze of questions with no answers. Something very bad had happened, I reasoned, and my hero, John, was right smack in the middle of it.

I thought, "Boys can't switch into being girls. Can they?"

John was the apple of my eye. When he straddled me atop his shoulders and traipsed through the rooms of our house, I felt ten feet tall. There was a special chemistry between my brother and me that would always transcend time.

*Daddy with C.D., who as a 14-year-old drove
the family in a rented car to Parris Island, S.C.*

Chapter 2

In for Some Hard Times

"She cried all the way to her new home."

June 19, 1931, is a Sunday laced with unforgettable memories. Mama and seven of her eight children had stayed home that day.

After preaching that morning at Pleasant Valley Baptist Church on the outskirts of Waycross, Daddy and my brother Skeet, who was eleven, went home for Sunday dinner with a family from his church. After the meal, the lady of the house gathered her own brood and Skeet and went to visit her sister.

Daddy and his deacon friend stood in the front doorway facing the yard. A gentle rain was falling. They were discussing how bad times were.

Daddy said, "We're in for some hard times. I have a wife and eight children. However, I believe that when a man has the will, a way will be made for him."

Suddenly the weather took a violent turn. No sooner had daddy uttered those words than lightning hit the outside radio grounding system. Electrical current sped from the grounding wires around the house and struck both men.

Daddy died instantly. His friend fell on top of him and survived to tell the story.

When Skeet, who idolized our daddy, returned to the farm site he went into shock. A crowd had gathered and was getting ready to rush the two men to the hospital. For Daddy, it was too late.

At first Mama refused to believe Daddy was dead. It was not until Skeet said, "Mama, it's true. Daddy is gone," that reality began to set in.

Mama, who like my daddy was thirty-one, in seconds became a widow with eight children and, although unknown at the time, was pregnant with another— and I was only four months old.

A community had lost a minister of great promise. The shocking news spread like a raging fire throughout the communities of rural South Georgia where it remained for years to come as a "Do you remember when?" topic of conversation.

Three years later my daddy's brother, Alfred, came calling. "Cleo," he said to Mama, "is it true the younger boys are picking up cigarette butts off the streets and smoking them?"

Mama didn't look up but nodded her head.

Alfred continued, "Ma, Pa, and I have been talking. We think the children, except the baby, should be sent to the new Baptist orphans home."

Mama burst into tears. "Alfred," she said, "surely you don't mean that. I've lost Ward, and now you want me to give up my children. Rest assured, I'll never give up my children."

Alfred left saying, "Think it over, Cleo. It's the right thing to do."

Bad news traveled fast. Mama's favorite brother, Crawley, came the next morning. He found Mama on the back porch, crying. He handed Mama his handkerchief, saying, "Cleo, stop crying and tell me what's wrong."

Mama told him, "Alfred wants to put my children in an orphans home. And if that weren't enough, the bank is taking our house because I can't come up with the mortgage payments."

Crawley, puffing away on his ever-present cigar, grew angry. "Cleo, that's a dirty shame. Why don't Ward's people pay off the mortgage?"

"Alfred claims they don't have the money. All he talks about is sending the children to the orphans home."

"Well, well," said Crawley, shifting from one foot to the other. "That bunch may not have money to help you, but they have plenty of money for new trucks."

He paused and then added, "At least there isn't any mortgage on your farm. Listen to me, Cleo. Don't worry about your children going to an orphans home. They'll never go. As long as there is a scrap of food in my house, you'll never go hungry."

Mama knew she could count on Crawley. What he said, he would do. Mama was now thirty-four, and her oldest child was sixteen. Her youngest, namely me, was three. She suffered a miscarriage at the time of Daddy's death.

Even so, the move from a small town to rural life was hard for Mama. She cried all the way to her new home. Instead of a few blocks she would be miles away from her beloved sister, Maude.

Chapter 3

Mama Makes Ambrosia

"A chubby five-foot lady with dancing green eyes…
holds center stage in this bleak setting."

Scarlett had her "Tara" and Ashley his "Twin Oaks." The Sweat family had "The Sycamores," and it was there I find my favorite Mama memories.

Travel down a flat, sandy road fifteen miles south of Waycross, Georgia, until you come to a cluster of sycamore trees. The structure belongs to the Early, Early-American or "Let's Get a Roof over Our Heads" era.

The unpainted six-room house has a porch across the front and down its left side. The outer wall of the living room is made of chinked-together logs. As you enter the house, its scant furnishings are evident.

There are two worn upright chairs, a small table, and on the wall a thirty-inch portrait of Daddy holding his Bible.

The door to the left of the living room leads to Mama's bedroom. Her iron bedstead with its two high-rise feathered mattresses is covered with a handmade Dutch Girl quilt. A massive long dresser made of ornate wood and housing a mirror stands against the wall.

Go back into the living room and through the door opposite the front door, and you're now in a pantry-size room. Like all of the rooms, its floors are bare and unpainted.

From here you enter the dining room, where two wooden benches offset its eight-foot plank table, covered in a red checkered oilcloth. Against the wall stands a wooden safe for baked goods.

The dining room opens into the kitchen where pine lighter knots, dipped in rosin, make the cast iron stove turn crimson.

A chubby, five-foot lady with dancing green eyes and a ready smile holds center stage in this bleak setting. She wears a flour-sack print dress and almost always has on an apron.

A widow with eight children, she is in perpetual motion. Whether baking doughnuts, wringing the neck of a chicken, standing guard over a cast iron wash pot filled with dirty clothes, washing down the front porch with a corn shuck mop, overseeing weekly baths in a zinc tub, chasing down and killing a huge rat snake, telling ghost stories that made you pee in your pants, or peddling away on her prized sewing machine, Mama knitted life into forever memories.

Mama, who as a child grew up being catered to, adjusted in her adult years to poverty and hard labor. No job was too demeaning if it would keep her family fed, clothed, and housed.

Modern conveniences during my childhood were what other people had—not us. Cleaning the globes and trimming the wicks of kerosene lamps, picking cotton in the blazing sun, canning, cooking on a wood stove—these were everyday "Mama" jobs.

Mama took what life dished out and turned it into ambrosia.

In the summer of my sixth year Mama heard of a W.P.A. government-sponsored program that was hiring women to sew. So, Mama rented out our farm to tenants and moved us three miles away to the tiny Haywood community. Getting the job, she commuted by train to Waycross for twenty cents each day roundtrip.

Soon Mama decided to move us again—this time back to Waycross. I felt like I'd died and gone to heaven. We had indoor plumbing. That meant no more long trips to an outdoor privy.

We even had a bathtub. It took Mama a while to get us a tub stopper, but that didn't keep my brothers or me from using the slanting back of the tub as a slide.

Mama hired a maid to stay with us in the afternoons and to cook our supper. Miss Essie had her hands full keeping us kids from squabbling.

Soon, living expenses exceeded our income and Miss Essie had to go. Then Mama's job became part time, and things for our family began spiraling downward.

By the time I was seven we had moved seven times. Landlords kept expecting to be paid, but we couldn't pay them.

No one in my family attended church anymore. Still, my thirst for God stories continued. In the middle of a very bleak year, grace lit upon me in the form of my schoolteacher and a very special Bible storybook.

One day the postman delivered a large box to our house. Mama opened it, and out spilled twenty Bible storybooks sent by my brother John in Atlanta.

Suddenly my eyes landed on a special book. "Mama, Mama," I exclaimed, "This is the book our teacher reads to us!"

I stopped Mama in her tracks and begged her to read it to me. From that day forward, when I got home from school the first thing I did was reread the story my teacher had read that afternoon.

I couldn't get enough of the stories of David slaying Goliath, Esther, Joseph, Ruth, Dorcas, and Peter. Especially appealing to me were the times when Jesus took little children in his arms and blessed them.

When I read how his enemies had treated Jesus, I cried. I left my book behind and went to the steps of our back porch. My seven-year-old thoughts went something like this: "Jesus, I'm sorry you had to die. I love you and I need you."

Time and time again I have moved in my thoughts to those back porch steps to remember a teacher who knew we needed more than reading, writing, and arithmetic, and a brother who in the midst of personal chaos wanted to share his heritage with his siblings.

Although our churchgoing days had ceased when we moved back into Waycross, those Bible storybooks kept my God-hunger alive.

Mama

Chapter 4

Her Tarnished Halo

"Mama must have had her head in the sand and
her heart on her sleeve…"

Like Route 66, the year 1939 seems never to end. We had moved a dozen times when we arrived at Margaret Street in Old Nine, the poorest residential section of Waycross. Mama's job was non-existent now, and there were five of us children still at home.

In those so-called "good old days" there was no city, state, or national help for poor families. However, we did get our share of grapefruit, grits, flour, and underwear that had a zillion buttons to undo.

On Margaret Street we were back to an outdoor privy and kerosene lamps. Our main diet consisted of fried potatoes, grits, hoecakes and fatback bacon.

When winter came, my brothers broke some of our already damaged chairs for kindling. When the chairs ran low, my brothers took turns sneaking outside and stealing wood stashed under our neighbor's house.

Daddy had been dead eight years when Mama found herself a beau—and none of us children were in an accepting mood. Her boyfriend, Joe, was a tall, balding man with a heavy body frame who liked to play the banjo. He was friendly and easy to talk with.

Hindsight reveals he had little desire to better himself economically. The jobs he held were either selling produce or serving as a night watchman. For some reason he never held a job for more than a few months at a time, even during World War II. Most of the time he had no job.

Mama must have had her head in the sand and her heart on her sleeve when she married a man with nine children, four of whom were still at home.

Perhaps Joe had more sinister motives. He was looking for a mother for his girls. If Mama married Joe thinking her life and ours would be more secure, she was in for a rude awakening.

Shortly after Mama and Joe's marriage in 1939 we moved to a seedy hotel on Plant Avenue in Waycross, where all fourteen of us occupied one long room. One low-wattage bulb was suspended from the ceiling. The bathing and toilet facilities were down the hall from our room and were used by all the tenants.

The room came unfurnished. Three iron posted beds took up most of the floor space. We slept four to a bed with no partitions between us.

Age-wise I fell between Joe's eight-year-old and ten-year-old daughters. At first we hit it off well. It was fun having built-in playmates. Then the usual pattern of not being able to pay the rent and having to move ensued.

During one of those journey stops—when I was in the fourth grade—two of my stepsisters and I climbed atop a lean-to shed in our backyard. Throwing a towel around my shoulders, I announced to the world I was Superman and sailed forth to right the world of its wrongs. A big thud followed my descent onto a mound of dirt. I got up smarting some sore muscles and a bruised ego.

Three children have seldom been known to form a lasting friendship pact. So it was with us. We hadn't been together long before tempers began to flare and territorial rights were staked. Joe's children took to Mama's warm, loving ways. I was in no mood to share Mama with these invaders.

A flurry of moves followed—back and forth to rental houses and apartments in Waycross—until now it makes my head spin trying to put the events of this portion of my life in some semblance of order.

Months elapsed and after moving every time the rent came due, Mama decided to move us back to the family farm where I would finish the fourth grade.

President Franklin D. Roosevelt was busy proposing sweeping legislation to boost our economic anemia and flagging spirits. One of his programs brought electricity to our farm. We still had an outdoor privy and drew water from a well, but we had electric lights!

I turned the front porch light off and on so many times that Mama threatened to spank me if I didn't quit. So I stopped. I knew a peach tree switch in her hands would become a lethal weapon.

Joe had convinced Mama to mortgage the farm to buy him a truck. That truck was supposed to work miracles and open up a whole new work world for us. He talked of selling produce all over north Florida. But his plan fizzled. He sold the truck, squandered the money, and Mama was left to pay off the mortgage years later when she sold her farm.

Our subscription to *The Atlanta Journal*, furnished by my brother John, opened the windows of my mind to the existence of racial bias. "The Wild Man of Sugar Creek" ruled politics in Georgia. Eugene Talmadge Senior owed his power to Georgia's infamous county unit system and his religious bias that the "Negra" was inferior to the white man.

Talmadge, his stringy hair flying and his red suspenders in full view, declared,

"I'm-a-standin' up to all the long hair, furrin' dictionary-swallowing sociologists from up North. Black's black and white's white, and never shall these twain meet. Naw sir!"

His logic and mine collided.

A swirl of dust came barreling down our dirt road in 1941, and I knew it must be our rural mail carrier. He came to a halt in front of the sycamore trees and beeped.

"Hello, Mr. Roy," I said. "Do you have any mail for us?'

He smiled and handed me a letter from my brother John along with *The Atlanta Journal.* Then he added, "Would you like a sucker?"

"Thank you, sir," I said as I ran toward the house. I gave Mama the letter from John, commenced licking on my sucker, and started looking for the funnies. The daily delivery of news out of Atlanta and a static-plagued radio were welcomed invaders to my isolated South Georgia world.

Since 1939 I'd listened to grownups talk of war in Europe. Under a mustached madman, Adolph Hitler, Germany was determined to rule the world. First they took Poland. It was almost certain France could not hold out against them much longer. Night after night the German air power pelted England with bombs.

"Mama," I asked, "what will we do if the Germans come to America?"
"We're better off than the people who live in the big cities," she said. "Maybe we could hide out in the woods."

In my dreams I saw zooming airplanes bearing a strange-looking mark called a "swastika." The enemy guns were aimed at churches, factory buildings, and houses.

Meanwhile, my sixteen-year-old brother, Harold, was hanging out all night at filling stations. He had quit school, chosen unsavory friends, and then decided to join the Marine Corps.

We received a telegram:

December 20, 1939, Collect 36 cents
Got in the Marines okay. Love, Harold

After he finished boot camp at Parris Island, South Carolina, there was talk of his unit being sent overseas. He wrote begging us to come.

There was just one hitch. We had no mode of transportation, not even a horse and wagon. How could we go to Parris Island, 150 miles away? None of us, except Mama on her wedding night, had ever been outside our county.

Someone hit upon the idea of renting a car. My brother, John, now living in Atlanta, immediately wired Mama the money for it. My fourteen-year-old brother, C. D., became the designated driver. This presented a potential problem, since his only driving experience had been in my uncle's cow pasture.

We motored along without any mishaps and in four hours arrived at Parris

Island. Military police carrying guns stopped us at the entrance gate and informed us they would send for my brother. We pulled into the visitors' parking lot and waited. Soon my brother came, and we ate our picnic lunch.

Afterward we drove to Savannah, Georgia, thirty miles away, where Mama bought several hundred-pound sacks of chicken feed and we visited with a cousin.

Mama decided to stay in Savannah while the rest of us went home with our youthful, inexperienced, and unlicensed driver. All went well until we hit Thornton's Creek, a mile and a half from our farmhouse.

It was three o'clock in the morning. BANG! BANG! Down went a front tire. Like a rapid-firing machine gun, the other tires died of natural causes. There we were with four flat tires in the middle of nowhere in a rented car whose trunk was laden with chicken feed.

We crawled out of the car, all five of us, and walked home—leaving the car and chicken feed to fend for themselves.

A couple of weeks later, someone towed the car back to the rental company. Those were the days: we weren't charged an extra rental fee and even if they had charged us, we didn't have the money with which to pay it.

Chapter 5

Knight in Shining Armor

"While others in my senior class concentrated on diagramming sentences,
I struggled with topics such as…lobotomies."

On a late summer afternoon in 1941, John came home from Atlanta. Mama had warned us: "John is sick. Don't expect him to play games. He has a lot on his mind."

There were gosh-awful whispers about a newspaper account involving police-men raiding a homosexual ring at the YMCA, after which John had spent a night in jail and been fingerprinted.

I took one look and decided someone was mixed up. John looked fine to me! I leaped in the air and grabbed him around the neck. "Swing me round and round," I begged.

John obliged, but I could tell his heart wasn't in it.

Most of the time he was deathly quiet, a mere shadow of his usual talkative self. John did share with me the mysteries locked in his stage trunk: a rubber cigar, a score to a Broadway musical, fake eyeglasses, and his beloved tap dancing shoes.

Sometimes he placed candles on the mantle above our fireplace and lit them. When I asked him about the candles he told me he was praying.

I liked the lighted tapers, and thought they were a clever way to get God's attention. I enjoyed watching the flickering flames cast shadows on the dark walls.

He wasn't home long, not even two weeks, when his boss wrote and John returned to Atlanta.

But in a few months he was back home again, this time to stay. Our family, what was left of it at that point, now lived in Jacksonville, Florida, where I was a struggling sixth-grader. John, obviously depressed, had quit work and did not seek employment. To make matters worse, he and our stepfather were at loggerheads.

Months went by and then one afternoon John came in and announced:

"Guess what? You're looking at a Marine. I leave Friday for boot camp at Parris Island, South Carolina!"

Mama and I were both thrilled and shocked. We felt this was a make-or-break situation for John. Mama's understanding of homosexuality and other issues of gender identification was little better than mine—and I had none.

At Parris Island, John made an excellent recruit. Thanks to President Franklin D. Roosevelt's new ruling, he was placed in a casual platoon, meaning the training wasn't as rigorous as it had once been for recruits. John received commendation from his drill sergeant and got a medal for his sharp-shooting abilities. He was given an aptitude test that showed him well suited for clerical duties. John wrote home:

> I've been picked to be in the Marine Honor Guard in Washington, D.C. Our drill team of which I am a member will perform when heads of states from around the world visit with our president. Isn't that exciting? I'm now a PFC.
>
> Love, John

Though John was very happy about being chosen to serve in the nation's capital, he was only in Washington for six months or less. My knowledge at this point is sketchy. I know only that at some point he was sent to Saint Elizabeth's Hospital in Bethesda, Maryland, a huge military hospital.

Shortly thereafter, Mama received a letter telling her the Marine Corps had given John an honorable medical discharge and she needed to come get him. Mama and my stepfather went up and brought him back to Jacksonville.

John was totally disoriented mentally, and was nothing but a bag of bones physically. His body was hunched over, and he looked like a very old man. I hardly recognized him.

When I was in the seventh grade a new treatment for mental illness called electroshock therapy was being tested in the United States. John, at the expense of the Marine Corps, went to a private facility five miles from home where he stayed for more than a month.

He seemed to make remarkable progress. However, after he got back home, he began to show signs of a relapse.

Mama had other challenges, however. With great moral courage she filed for a divorce from Joe. No one in her family had ever been divorced, and Mama didn't relish the distinction of being the first.

In today's climate it is hard to imagine the stigma once tied to being a divorced woman in the South where family unity—even when faked poorly —was highly valued.

On her own and mostly by telephone, Mama talked with realtors about selling her farmstead and buying a two-story house back in Waycross, Georgia, some seventy-five miles northwest of Jacksonville.

Prior to my thirteenth birthday, John, Mama, and I moved to Waycross, the city of our beginnings. Soon, my sister who had been living and working in Orlando, Florida, returned home too.

Generally speaking, things were looking up in 1944. Mama was able to easily rent her extra rooms to military personnel. And she and I were regulars in Sunday school and worship.

At age thirteen I made a public profession of my faith in Jesus Christ at Central Baptist Church in Waycross, and was baptized by Pastor Durwood V. Cason, who later worked to bridge relationships between white and black Baptists in Georgia.

But my brother John became worse instead of better. Finally, Mama had no recourse but to have him institutionalized. The closest veterans hospital for the mentally ill was in Augusta, Georgia, 150 miles from Waycross.

John stayed in the Augusta hospital for several years. His condition deteriorated to the point he didn't even recognize us when we went for a visit. Patients at the hospital who were doing well were put on unlocked wards. Those with severe problems were placed on locked wards. John was locked away.

In 1948, when I was sixteen, a new brain surgery was gaining credibility in America. Mom returned from visiting John with serious news. The doctors at the veterans hospital were recommending a surgery called a lobotomy.

The V.A. doctor explained to Mama: "If the surgery is successful, John will come out of it with a changed personality. He will be rational, but totally unlike his former self."

"What if I don't agree to the operation?" asked Mama.

"He will continue to get worse," said the doctor. "We admit this surgery is like playing pin-the-tail-on-the-donkey, but in John's case he's deteriorating rapidly."

Mama told the doctor she'd talk it over with her family and let the hospital have her answer soon. Our options seemed limited. Would we look on while John slowly died before our eyes, or would we gamble on an uncertain future for him?

We all agreed that the John we had once known and loved was already gone. Maybe, just maybe, the lobotomy would bring good results. Eventually we gave our approval for the surgery.

While others in my senior class concentrated on diagramming sentences, I struggled with topics such as being queer, mental illness, and lobotomies.

Still, no adults talked with me about any of these topics. By now, I'd pieced together some "facts" of my own—albeit woefully wrong.

The lobotomy changed John's entire personality, making him excessive in everything he said or did. We soon learned that if he said black was white, then the best thing to do was to agree with him. Trying to reason with him was a lesson in futility.

While John was obnoxious and often offensive after his lobotomy, he was never physically dangerous.

The part that never changed about John was his sexual orientation. He had gone to Atlanta as a young gay man. He left Atlanta as a gay man, entered the United States Marine Corps as a gay man, and was medically discharged from the United States Marine Corps as a gay man. He went through a series of electro-shock treatments and had a prefrontal lobotomy. None of these things changed his sexual orientation. He died in his fifties from a stroke.

I have a typewritten note from Hattie McDaniel to John dated March 12, 1940, thanking him for a letter he sent praising her performance as Mammy in *Gone with the Wind*. She closed the letter in her own handwriting: "Thanking you for your kind letter I am very truly yours, Hattie McDaniel."

From the time I was seven until the time John died in 1978, when I was forty-seven, I wrestled intellectually, spiritually, and emotionally with his sexual orientation and mental illness. How could a life with so much promise end up with so much sorrow?

Although I grappled to understand the causes, my search always left me baffled. I loved my brother, and wanted desperately to see him change.

John had been my knight in shining armor. So, when John lost his way mentally, my entire family suffered—mentally, physically, and emotionally. If I had known then what I know now, I'd have been a better sister and friend to my brother John.

Chapter 6

Family Fragmentation

"Mama's marriage had done more than an orphans home
could ever have done to disintegrate our family."

A couple of years after Mama and Joe split, he came for his girls and moved them to Jacksonville, Florida. Another year came and went before Joe talked Mama into joining him in Florida.

In the meantime my sister Kathryn and I were dumped on my father's parents in the Forks of the Hurricane to spend the summer of '42. I was eleven.

To my sister, a teenager, it felt like being assigned to Sing-Sing prison. She was unhappy and worked at being contrary.

I met my waterloo at a red clay embankment close to the house. I spent hours creating objects and in the meantime covered my body with clay.

The Sweat farmhouse was big and rambling. Branching off from the entrance hallway was the parlor, the "holy of holies." We were only allowed in the parlor if we had special permission. This hall of fame housed an upright piano and eight-by-ten portraits of the family.

Toward the end of summer we got a postcard saying Mama was on her way to get us.

All summer long Grandma had badmouthed Mama, but when she arrived, Grandma gave her a royal welcome. As we packed to leave, my sister began telling Mama all the things Grandma had said. Grandma, who had been eavesdropping, entered the room raving.

She threatened to beat my sister with a broom handle if she didn't take back the things she told Mama. My sister, true to form, didn't recant and we left Grandma's on shaky ground.

Mama told us we were moving to Jacksonville. She might as well have told us we were moving to Timbuktu, West Africa, or Shanghai, China. Jacksonville, seventy-five miles away, was, for us, a long way from The Sycamores.

Our new residence was a downstairs rental house on Jackson Street that abutted Riverside Drive, a busy thoroughfare. The two-storied, faded house stood close to the sidewalk. The barrenness of its outside was only exceeded by the mass of unanswered questions running rampant through my mind.

Within a week our family, for the first time, became fragmented. My brother Herbert, fifteen months my senior, refused to come with us. Instead he elected to stay with one of Mama's sisters and continued going to school. Later he joined our brother Skeet in Charleston, South Carolina.

World War II was in full bloom, and it wasn't long before my fourteen-year-old brother had quit school and taken employment with the Charleston U.S. Navy Ship Yard.

Harold was in the Marines, and C. D. worked at the Navy Yard in Portsmouth, Virginia.

My oldest sister had for a long time been employed as a grocery clerk at Jacksonville Beach. That left only my sister Kathryn and me at home. She enrolled in the eighth grade, but left in six weeks to live with a friend and got a job as a telephone operator.

Mama's marriage had done more than an orphans home could ever have done to disintegrate our family. I was now the only one of the children living at home; the rest of them were scattered afar.

Toss in the perils of World War II and my brother's sexual conflicts and you begin to see a family at war with itself.

Three blocks to the left of our rented house lay the sprawling, treacherous St. John's River. John often threatened to end his life by jumping into its murky depths.

Late one afternoon he said, "My life is a mess and I'm no good for anyone or anything. I'm going to the river and end it all."

I grabbed his arm and walked along with him as he barged toward the river. Once he broke away from me, and I thought for sure he was a goner.

I told him, "I love you. Please don't jump into the river." We stayed at the river's edge for a half hour. Slowly he turned and we returned home.

I'm straining to put Mama into that scene, but for some reason she isn't there. Did she ignore John's talk of suicide? Was she so wrapped up in her marital woes that she couldn't deal with her son's needs?

No one was talking things over, and it was certain no one talked with me—even though I was now twelve.

This became the beginning of a love-hate relationship between Mama and me. I didn't understand her. I didn't admire her. I continually wished she were someone else. My heart longed for security, acceptance, and laughter. To top it all, God seemed far removed.

An old nursery rhyme by Henry Wadsworth Longfellow reflects my rebellious teen years.

> There was a little girl,
>> Who had a little curl,
> Right in the middle of her forehead.
>> When she was good,
>> She was very good indeed,
> But when she was bad, she was horrid.

In 1945 Mama married for a third time and we moved to Savannah. When my newly acquired stepfather Cecil insisted that I quit school in the tenth grade and go to work, I exploded, venting my frustrations on Mama.

"Hell, no!" I said, screaming and running to my bedroom. "I'll be damned if I'll quit school and go to work. I'll go live with Daddy's sister. I hope I never lay eyes on you again."

Mama must have been distressed at my outbursts. However, I don't remember her trying to talk me out of going. Instead she wrote my daddy's sister and told her what I wanted to do. My aunt, who had a daughter one year younger than I, readily agreed.

So, as a sixteen-year-old high school junior, I left home. I rode the Greyhound bus from Savannah to Waycross, where my sister and her boyfriend met and drove me to my aunt's home in Pierce County.

As I look back, I'm convinced my relatives worked at making me feel a part of their family. The truth is, I was so consumed with love-hate feelings toward Mama and my step-father that I was incapable of giving or receiving love.

A challenging childhood led to a lifetime of lessons.

I stayed a few months and then went to live with my eldest sister and her husband in Jacksonville. My enrollment in a gigantic school complex did nothing to boost my sagging ego, and I spent my days wallowing in self-pity.

Finally I told Mama I was ready to come back home to Savannah. My stepfather never again mentioned that I should quit school and go to work. Nevertheless, I continued to hold a super grudge against him.

At church I was mannerly, a serious Bible student, willing to serve, and fervent in my prayers. It's a good thing the church crowd didn't peek in on me when I was performing one of my mouth attacks at home.

At age seventeen I graduated as part of the class of '48 at Savannah's Commercial High School. Then it was back to Jacksonville, where I was halfway hunting for a job but really wanting to go to college. A restless God-hunger continued to gnaw at me.

Chapter 7

Traces of the Divine

"...She never got over her God-hungers."

One may think that some of the things that have occurred in my life were pure happenstance. That wouldn't include me. I prefer to call them traces of the divine.

Two such incidents involve the arrival of *Letters from Aunt Charlotte* and a preacher's wife in Jacksonville.

There were plenty of Bible storybooks on the market in the 1930s, but what are the chances the title of one of the books—*Letters from Aunt Charlotte*—would match the copy my teacher was reading to her second grade class at school? And who could have known the profound effect that particular book would have on my life?

It is as if God heard a little seven-year-old girl's love words and in return took hold of her with an everlasting love. And even though there were many times when she was unaware of God's nearness, she never got over her God-hungers.

My rebellious nature had pretty much subsided by the time I graduated from high school. God got my attention and gave me a burning desire to become an international missionary—and then shocked me with the news I'd have to go to college for four years and then obtain a master's degree in religious education.

Money was scarce, and job opportunities were limited. I took on two temporary jobs, but when they fizzled, once again I went looking for work around Jacksonville. But then, a miracle was about to happen.

A pastor's wife named Leona Althoff had worked her way through college and wanted me to do the same. One thing led to another. And before I knew it I had been accepted at Mary Hardin-Baylor, a Baptist college for women in Belton, Texas, and was headed west on a Greyhound bus.

Belton in 1949 looked like a deserted boon town. The bus station was no exception. After a twenty-hour bus ride I plopped down in the first chair I saw and looked around. No one was there to meet me, and grasshoppers that seemed to be three feet long were hopping all over me.

I checked my money. The twenty-five dollars in my billfold weren't enough to get me back home. I had to make this work.

As I pondered the pitiful mess I was in, some fellows came and escorted me to my dormitory. The rest is history.

I sat down in the middle of my room and started unpacking. Someone with a Texas drawl and great big smile popped in and said, "I'm Pat Lockridge. Who are you?"

I told her my name and she said, "Well, girl, come on; it's time for dinner. Do you have a pair of stockings?"

I started fumbling through my suitcase. It must have taken me too long because she added, "Come on, girl. They don't like for us to be late. They won't say anything about the stockings since you just arrived."

Pat went with me to dinner and stayed with me through the stunt night events that followed. I went to bed that night knowing one thing was certain: I was home. It was as if a long search was over.

Was it heaven on earth? Are you kidding?

Pat worked six hours each day in the infirmary taking care of sick people, mopping, cleaning urinals, and so on. My job was in the dining hall, and I worked four hours a day scraping and washing dishes, serving as a waitress, or polishing silver.

My freshman English teacher frightened me to death. I had her for at least two semesters, and my fear never ceased. She was a no-nonsense person who left someone like me with the jitters.

Perhaps, I thought, speech as a major will even things up. After all, I'd written two essays and my church friends thought I was very good at public speaking. That didn't work either. English I was stuck with but with speech out, I had no major.

Then there were those classes in Spanish. Unfortunately for me, I got thrown into a class of advanced students. While I struggled to say, "*Buenos dias,*" they were conjugating sentences.

Somewhere in this sea of Texans, however, was a teacher from Pine Mountain, Georgia. She had a deep bass voice and when she sang, "God Leads His Dear Children Along," everyone on campus took note.

It wasn't long before Pat and I decided that whatever she was teaching was where we wanted to be.

Growing up in South Georgia, I used to hear grown-ups describe certain individuals as being "as ugly as homemade sin." Even as a child I knew that homemade sin was as ugly as it got. Some folk may have described Marguerite "Doc" Woodruff as being ugly as homemade sin. I wouldn't.

Marguerite had crystal blue eyes, a gutsy laugh, and a corner-to-corner smile.

However, very thick lips marred her facial features. The longer you knew her, the less attention you paid to her facial features.

She had little trouble convincing seven others and me that a major in sociology was a perfect fit for someone going into missions.

Doc was patient with my limitations and overlooked my brashness. Seeing me through the eyes of Christ, she was able to challenge me to become a real learner, not for just one course but for life.

Marguerite "Doc" Woodruff

The eight of us who became her first majors were a motley crew. One had been thrown out of her home when she switched from being a member of the Church of Christ to being a Baptist, two were Chinese refugees, and one was from Hawaii. The biggest thing we had in common was our love for Doc.

She returned our devotion tenfold. She took us to conventions, had picnics with us, taught our Sunday school class, and was an integral part of our Baptist Student Union activities.

We all thought one circumstance was grossly unfair. Although Doc was an excellent sociology teacher, her training had been in theology. In the 1950s this put her in a class by herself.

She was the only female doctoral student of the legendary Christian ethicist T. B. Maston at Southwestern Baptist Theological Seminary and the first woman to earn such a degree from a Southern Baptist institution. Why wasn't she teaching theology and Christian ethics somewhere?

There is one simple explanation: Marguerite Woodruff was a woman. I'm sorry to say we can't lay the blame on the latter-day fundamentalist Southern Baptists. In the 1950s they were not in charge.

What Doc did for me enriched my life long after college days ceased. She taught me by example that being a female is a blessing, not a curse. Because of her, I began to accept personal responsibility for racial injustice. The fire she lit in my heart to know truth and to express love in tangible ways still burns.

Chapter 8

Strong Women

"It isn't where you start out that counts but rather where you end up."

The timely presence of strong women is a common thread woven throughout my story. The immeasurable, deep-shaping influence of crucial people at critical points in my personal journey cannot be overstated.

Leona Althoff taught youth Sunday school at Ortega Baptist Church in Jacksonville, Florida, near the Naval Air Station. The church was experiencing growing pains but had just built a new brick parsonage (or "pastorium," as we called it). The youth would meet in the kitchen since Leona, the pastor's wife, was our teacher.

Sixty years later I'm having trouble conjuring up even her facial features. I do remember she was tall, wore glasses, and was soft spoken and witty.

I had graduated from high school in Savannah and moved back to Jacksonville. As the younger generation would say, I was CON-fused. The only thing in the world that appealed to me was becoming a missionary. And to do that, I would need more education than I could afford. I had no desire to get a job, even though my purse was empty.

There I was this almost-eighteen-year-old teenager from Savannah who for the second time in less than two years was living with her oldest sister in Jacksonville. My sister kept circling ads in the newspaper and furnishing me with bus fare. I even followed through on a few of her suggestions. But my heart wasn't in getting a job, and to say my job-getting skills were inept is to beg the question.

So, back to Leona's kitchen table at the parsonage: During our Sunday school lesson at some point I expressed my dilemma about not having any money to go to college. Ms. Leona's face lit up. "What if I told you of a college where you could go and not pay a cent?"

We all giggled.

"Well, that's true," she said. "Instead of paying money, you work. It's hard but it can be done. I know it's true because I worked six hours a day for my education."

"Where is this school?" I asked.

"It's a Baptist girls school in Belton, Texas," said Leona. "Would you like for me to write the college and see if I can get you a work scholarship?"

I gave her the go signal and couldn't wait to get back home and talk it over with Mama and my former pastor at Immanuel Baptist Church in Savannah. My excuses had run out.

This was daring, it was big, and my heavenly father seemed to be saying, "This is my way for you. Go and I'll go with you."

Suddenly a big weight was lifted and I felt like dancing in the rain. Leona opened for me a door of opportunity. What had seemed impossible was now possible. To me this event is more than a happenstance. God was working in my behalf, removing a financial mountain and making a way for me to attend college.

Pat Lockridge Shannon was the first person to welcome me to Mary Hardin-Baylor College. She was also on work scholarship.

Pat worked six hours a day in the infirmary with no support from her parents, who weren't happy over her being in college. At least I was only working four hours a day in the dining hall. My sisters and their husbands helped me some financially while Mama kept me in clothes and sent food care packages.

Pat and I were put in closer contact during our sophomore year when we both decided to become sociology majors under Dr. Marguerite Woodruff. We were drawn to Doc's warm friendly ways—and she was always taking us on special trips.

Just before we graduated from college, Pat became engaged to some guy from Baylor University by the name of John Shannon. After graduation we lost touch with each other.

Many years later when my son Alan decided to attend Baylor, my thoughts returned to Pat. We exchanged several letters.

I learned that Pat had three children and had taught school in France while her husband worked as a civil service accountant before returning to Texas.

When I attended a Baylor football game against the Texas Longhorns, Pat and John stopped by for breakfast on their way to Tullahoma, Oklahoma, to have Thanksgiving with John's family. Shortly thereafter, Pat invited Alan to her home for the weekend.

Our next encounter was Mary Hardin-Baylor's thirty-year reunion for the class of '53. I hadn't been to the campus since graduation. It was kind of like going home again. One thing was certain: It wouldn't take me thirty more years before I'd return to my alma mater again. On my second reunion trip Pat and I shared a motel room.

When my husband died in 1994, I was going through a list of people to call and Pat's name emerged. From that time forward we reconnected more often. Pat would meet my plane in Austin and drive me to her home in Killeen—where I had my own upstairs getaway with a private bath.

After her husband John died, the bond between us grew deeper. Pat's life has solidified my conviction that it isn't where you start out that counts but rather where you end up.

Marguerite Woodruff and I were the only two Georgians at my college in Texas for some time. That created an instant bond between us, although we were from different parts of the state.

"Doc," as she preferred to be called, was my college advisor and instructor when I chose sociology as a major during my sophomore year.

I primed for my first test until I could have regurgitated its contents from memory. Test day came and went. I felt good about the results, thinking I had aced it. When I got my paper back my feathers drooped. I had a B-. According to Doc, I knew my material but had not amplified enough on the essay questions.

After that I often vacillated on my test answers. Sometimes I gave too much information. Doc was patient with my limitations and overlooked my brashness. Seeing me through the eyes of God, she was able to chisel away until I became a real student.

I had arrived at Mary Hardin-Baylor totally unprepared to take on the rigors of collegiate life academically or socially. They didn't offer remedial classes in those days. If they had, my name would have been at the top of the list.

What Doc did for me enriched my life long after college days ceased. She taught me by example that being a female is a blessing. She also lit a fire in my heart to search for truth and to express love in tangible ways.

Her life taught me not to major on bad experiences of the past but to break loose from them. Doc taught me to believe in myself, to never give up, and to soar like an eagle.

Then there was Mama. Archie Cleo Jordan Sweat Millikin Wallace, born in 1900, met my daddy when she was seventeen. They fell in love and two years later, in 1918, married.

Nothing in either of their backgrounds prepared them for the economic problems they would face during the Great Depression era. Fourteen years later, in 1931, at age thirty-one, she faced being a widow with eight children to nurture. I was just four months old.

Yet Mama bequeathed me the gifts of laughter, love of a good story, integrity, devotion to family, the nobility of hard work, and a do-or-die spirit.

Laden with cares, Mama always found or created an occasion to evoke laughter. My eyes see her now, her head tossed back in riotous laughter. If I listen closely, I still hear her calling me to never take myself too seriously.

Mama was a natural when it came to storytelling. When she was sure she had your undivided attention, she was at her best. Mama would start out telling about something that supposedly happened, like being stopped by the state patrol for speeding. By the time she got through emoting, we were all doubled over laughing. Incidentally, the state patrol believed her wild tale and she got away without a ticket.

Integrity, if you have it, is what is left when you have blotched up your life and have to start all over again. Mama was taught by example as a child that a person's word is a person's bond, meaning when you promise to do something and shake hands, it becomes as binding as a legal matter. Later in life Mama entered many contracts, but in her heart of hearts the handshake was all she really needed. Mama had integrity.

Mama's do-or-die spirit was well tested. When left with a marriage that crumbled, she started all over again. She made decisions concerning my brother John's destiny that no woman should have to make alone.

Mama seemed to learn from every experience, bad or good, she encountered. During Mama's third marriage, while I was in college, she was forced to choose between her husband and two mentally ill sons, my oldest brother John and the brother next to me age-wise, Herbert. Mama, with her own unique savvy, was able to salvage both. She bought a big apartment house, kept her sons at home, and rented out apartments. At the same time she maintained a healthy, if limited, relationship, with her third husband.

The gift I treasure most from Mama was her generous heart. Mama loved to give gifts to others, and she often gave when she needed the money for herself. Her gifts of food, money, and items made with her hands or rescued from an "On Sale" table were numerous. Giving was integral to who Mama was.

Much of my teen and young adult years found me locked in a love-hate relationship with Mama. By the time I'd married and had a child of my own, the hate part had vanished.

Once I penned to her the following message:

Dear Mama,

As the calendar moves forward, I look for the woman I am becoming in the child you nurtured.
    You have left your marks on me, and I am forever in your debt.
    Among these marks are your response to adversity, the nobility of honest work, your insistence that life be lived in the present tense, your belief that religion and pretend don't mix, and your super abundance of laughter and caring.
    Mama, I've watched as problems piled up on you until they reached insurmountable odds, only to see you defy them one by one. Whether it was a lack of money, broken love promises, or heartache stacked upon heartache, you always found room to laugh and love.

I remember seeing you hovering over a wash pot of clothes and watching you hang its contents up to dry—line upon line of overalls and dresses.

I watched as you wrung a chicken's neck, plucked its feathers, and cooked up a batch of yummy chicken and dumplings.

In my mind's eye I see you pushing a heavy cornhusk mop, or putting a cast iron to work on a mountain of clothes. Whatever had to be done, you did it.

Cooking was/is your specialty. Others in the family would have gingerbread for supper. Not me. Gingerbread boy would soon pop out of the oven and become my sole property. Yum-yum.

I liked to watch your feet pumping up and down on our treadle sewing machine. You made me dresses from suit samples and floral flour sacks.

Mama, I've never thought of you as a great theologian, but that only shows my bias. You never had any use for people who used religion wrongly. I can count the times I've heard you gossip or "bad mouth" others. You showed me, by your example, that pretend and religion are a bad mix.

You, who knew so much sorrow, could have closed the book on the present and the future. Lately your doctor reports your heart is enlarged. That's not news to me. Mama, your heart has always been enlarged. You are constantly finding ways to share. Family, friends, neighbors, and renters receive from your generous, enlarged heart.

Mama, I love you. Happy Mother's Day!

—Lynelle Mason
Rossville, Georgia
1970

The week preceding Mama's death was very tense. We knew and she knew that death was imminent. We were blessed with several lucid days, however. I promised to take her longhaired Chihuahua home with me, and to do the best I could for my emotionally disturbed brother, Herbert. John had died several years before Mama's illness.

Then her case worsened. That's when I got my first foretaste of what it is like to make a hard, irreversible decision. The doctor told us if Mama lived, she would be on a respirator for the rest of her life and would have to go to a rest home. Our other option was to take her off the respirator and let her die naturally.

Mama had a horror of going to a rest home. Existing, to her, especially in a rest home, would not be living. My sisters and I opted to take her off the respirator, and Mama died several hours later. Most families, when they have a death, only plan the services and interment. My sisters and I had something more urgent to do.

We made plans to have our brother Herbert put in a private mental clinic. He would not go peacefully, so we had to obtain a letter from his psychologist, have it approved by the court, and get a policeman to take him to the clinic.

Then we rallied the troops and, according to Mama's request, had a memorial service at her home church, and then drove seventy-five miles, had a closing service, and buried her body between John Jr. and her first husband, John Ward Sweat Sr.

At the memorial service in Savannah I asked to speak a few words and said:

Eternity

Cleo, get up. Get up and come home with me.
Cleo, get up. You are now free.

Free from breath that would not come,
Free from a heart grown sluggish ,
Free from the burdens of earthbound cares,
Free from loneliness and isolation,
Free from gnarled and twisted limbs.

Cleo, get up. Get up and come home with me,
Cleo, get up. Today you are truly free.

Free to enjoy heaven's bounty,
Free to rejoice with those whose journey preceded yours,
Free to forever serve and adore the Lord Jesus,
Free to wait at heaven's gate — waiting, waiting,
Until God, one by one, calls each of us to meet you there.

Come, Cleo, come on home.

My relationship with Mama matches that of many other females. In my childhood Mama could do no wrong, but by the time I became a teenager Mama could do no right.

At that stage of my life I was constantly wishing she were this vision I held of the perfect mother. Gradually, and after being affirmed of my own worth, I began to accept and love Mama as she was—with no strings attached.

When anyone today sees in me glimpses of generosity, a good work ethic, love of family, and laughter—they need to know these were gifts bequeathed to me by Mama.

Lynelle and Mama

Chapter 9

No Free Lunch

"...Self-esteem is fragile, and good deeds can sometimes
be perceived as a humiliation."

As a child, clad in hand-me-down clothes and forced to move often, I found it difficult to concentrate on tasks at school. I was poor, very poor. But I didn't want anyone else to know it or to feel sorry for me.

When I was in the second grade my teacher drew an outline of my bare foot in front of the entire class. Some lady was going to buy me a pair of shoes so I could be in the May Pole dance. She meant well, but even today when I recall it, my face gets red and I can hear the snickers of my classmates.

Another teacher gave me a free lunch ticket, which I really needed. Since the free tickets were a different color from those of the children who paid their fare, I conveniently lost mine in the restroom during recess.

Of course, someone reported what I had done to the teacher. But she didn't scold me and until this day, I hold her in high esteem.

Amid the accolades and affirmations life has brought me, I still find traces of low self-esteem surfacing. They send me, "You can't do that" messages. When they appear, I now hear an urgent voice saying, "Yes, you can. Go for it."

During my thirty years of teaching I never embarrassed a child because he lived on the wrong side of the tracks or lacked the common necessities of life. If a child needed help, I saw that he or she got it without anyone else in the class knowing.

I'm glad I learned early on that self-esteem is fragile and that good deeds can sometimes be perceived as a humiliation.

My love affair with working in Vacation Bible School started in the 1940s when I was fifteen and ended in 2009. I must have worked in a hundred of them through the years.

As a fifteen-year-old, I attended VBS in the mornings. Then on Sunday afternoons I taught a group of children and adults at a mission church of the Savannah Baptist Association.

In the 1940s and 1950s, Vacation Bible School was more structured than it is today. Children and their leaders marched behind the American and Christian flags, with a Bible bearer in the middle. The opening service included pledges to the flags and the Bible, with each pledge followed by a verse of Scripture and a song.

Some phase of Christian missions was spotlighted and an offering taken, after which the younger children departed. Then the VBS principal told a character story to the older children. The group also sang an anthem and recited a larger Scripture passage.

We accomplished all of this within a specific time frame, and the piano told us through chords when to sit and when to stand. Oftentimes the Bible schools lasted for two weeks.

My first paying job in college was with the Invincibles, a group of fifty or more students whose mission was to blanket the state of Texas with Vacation Bible Schools during the summer. Our name—coupled with our theme song "Got Any Rivers?"—was revealing.

We were convinced that with God's help we would make a difference. Saturdays were always moving days. I remember our first week on the field when my partner and I were left in an open area near the road with our luggage waiting for someone in a truck to pick us up. We waited and we waited. The heat waves of Texas were getting to me.

Just when we were about to give up, someone came. Upon arriving at our new living quarters, the family had lunch waiting. They'd been told we liked fried chicken. So for the entire week we had chicken—morning, noon, and night. When we arrived at the one-room church the following morning we were informed that our helpers had backed out. One by one we cornered the ladies, thrusting a VBS manual in their hands and extracting a promise that they'd try teaching for at least one day.

That little scene was repeated over and over for the next three years. We knew once they tried teaching, the ladies would keep coming. Never once did we have to forfeit a school.

I was learning a lot on the sidelines as well. When a sandstorm came whirling through, we were rushed to the house cellar. Upon returning upstairs we discovered about three inches of sand on the windowsills. To my Texas friends this was common, but to this Georgia peach it was a sight for sore eyes.

Most of the churches we served existed on a financial shoestring. However, one of our schools was held in a church with a working oil pump. On Wednesday nights during dry spells the people prayed for rain. One of their favorite lines was,

"Are you praying for rain? Where's your umbrella?"

The racial separate-but-equal clause in public education got my attention when we were assigned to clean out a one-room school for black children. There were no steps leading to the door. The books were outdated and the covers stripped.

When we attempted to move the teacher's desk, it collapsed. The entire area of the small school was layered with sand. As civil rights issues moved to the front burner of national politics, I never forgot what separate-but-equal really meant in many southern states.

Those three summers became the building blocks of my later careers. They gave me on-the-job training. Any future successes can be traced back to those hot Texas summers long ago.

At the end of my senior year I bought a plane ticket and returned to Savannah in high style, or so I thought. Awaiting me in Savannah was a teaching position at Moore Avenue Elementary School. My future plans included teaching for a year to pay off my $700 student loan, and then returning to Texas to study at the Baptist seminary in Fort Worth.

My teaching salary for that year was $150 a month. When I subtracted my tithe, the student loan payment, and $40 rent to Mama, I had little money left. But I inherited a well-behaved class of fifth graders and, to my credit, kept them that way.

When I stopped by the teacher's lounge after my first day, the principal said, "I wish I had a camera. I'd like to capture that beam on your face. It's priceless." I hadn't been ready for college, and I was unprepared to teach. I knew nothing about phonics or teaching reading. On the other hand, I was excellent in critical reading skills and social studies. The children, most of whom were good readers, didn't suffer.

In hindsight I get uncomfortable when I think how blatantly I ignored the separation of church-and-state issues. My Bible stories were long, and when I became the Girls in Action leader at my home church I easily recruited most of the girls in my class.

In 1954 I was still holding to my dream of becoming an international missionary or, as we phrased it in those days, a "foreign missionary." With that in mind and after teaching one year, I entered Southwestern Baptist Theological Seminary where I earned a master's degree in religious education.

I spent my summers during my seminary time under the direction of the Southern Baptist Home Mission Board. My first assignment was to the greater San Francisco area. Don't think this was a gig where I did a lot of sightseeing and little work. That wasn't the way it worked.

Since I was contemplating a career in missionary work, the board wanted to see how I'd handle a situation without having a partner. During my first week I

Southern Baptist students spread across Texas to assist churches and lead Vacation Bible Schools. Lynelle stands in the second row from the top, under the "O" in the banner.

shared a converted army barracks with a couple who had a little girl. Nothing had been done in preparation for the Bible school, and a mound of dirty dishes greeted me in our cramped living quarters. At nighttime I shared a cot with the couple's child.

Despite our uncomfortable surroundings, we enrolled 84 youngsters in Vacation Bible School. The pastor and his wife were pleasantly shocked. I had to move on to another location, but they continued the work there for another week.

Upon graduating from seminary in 1956, I was assigned by the Home Mission Board to the Oregon-Washington region. During orientation training in Portland, I learned that along with a girl from Alabama I'd been selected to work in Canada. After working for two weeks locally, my partner and I traveled by train through the beautiful Canadian Rockies for a one-week stay in Kamloops, British Columbia.

A doctor and his wife were on vacation in the States and left us the run of their house. Wow! One week was way too short for such luxuries. My partner and I spent the rest of our summer on Army cots with meager provisions in Saskatoon, Saskatchewan.

With seminary and Vacation Bible School experiences near and far behind me, I returned to Savannah to live with Mama and to teach at the same school where I'd taught before. I was also enlisted for the unpaid position of youth director at Morningside Baptist Church.

When I moved to Savannah as a youth in the late 1940s, the church was housed in a white frame building. By 1956 it was a towering brick structure boasting space for 700 or more in Sunday school.

It fell my lot to secure a speaker for the church's youth sweetheart banquet. So I invited "Doc" Woodruff, who was now chair of the sociology department at Mercer University in Macon, Georgia. I remember her reciting "The Hound of Heaven" by Francis Thompson.

As she spoke, I could see someone running away from God's calling and being forever hounded with "what might have been" thoughts. She spent the night at our home, and that's when I learned the church where she was a member, Tattnall Square Baptist Church, located on the campus of Mercer University, was looking for a minister of education.

Before Doc left, I'd agreed to be contacted by Tattnall Square's search committee. I subsequently moved from the classroom to serving as minister of education.

Now, to digress a bit, some of my passion for missions came from attending conferences at Ridgecrest Baptist Assembly in Western North Carolina—my first trip being as a high school senior in 1948. Attending YWA week at Ridgecrest was my reward for coming in second in a speaker's tournament in Savannah.

Baptist missionary M. Theron Rankin had been captured by the Japanese and imprisoned for nine months. I hung on to every word the missionaries said.

Chester Swor, known for inspiring generations of youth, urged us to "Take along a little honey," in challenging us to look for simple ways to share our faith. When I got home the first thing Mama said was, "I can tell you've changed."

Many factors were at play in shaping my calling. My various summer mission experiences convinced me I was an effective worker with children and had the ability to win the respect and assistance of church members and pastoral leaders. It never seemed like work that had to be done. It was demanding and consuming, but oh, how I loved it!

By the end of my first year of teaching public school I felt confident that someday, somewhere I'd be teaching children. During my final year at Southwestern Seminary during mission day services I tried to solidify my "calling." No specific field came; I felt called to all of them.

After my seminary days were over when I returned to Savannah and began looking for open doors, it didn't hurt that Morningside Baptist recognized and greatly encouraged my leadership skills. Soon my sense of missions became a call to education.

My own definition of being called into Christian service is expressed in this way: It was more a twining of the heart and mind; that God was inviting me to be a part of something bigger and better than I could imagine. If I trusted God with all my heart and soul, he would direct my way.

Therefore, I've had not *a* call but many calls—leading me to conclude Jesus has and is leading me all the way.

This is embarrassing to write, but it is indicative of my early sense of calling. When I was a sixteen-year-old member of the Girls Auxiliary, and declared my intention to my leaders and friends to become a missionary, I hadn't the foggiest idea what I was mouthing. My feathers fell when I read a pamphlet stating the high qualifications for a career missionary. I mean all that schooling might be well and good for someone else but frankly, I didn't need any additional training. God and I could handle anything, anywhere, anytime.

My naiveté continued at least through my freshman year at college. In those days I was going to become a missionary to Russia, probably the most forbidden country to Christians in the 1950s.

I don't demean the sense of my call during my teen years. Without that call I wouldn't have considered college and certainly not in far-off Texas. I still marvel that God never gave up on me. He continued to chip away at my brash spots and to encourage my soul longings.

My call to education was and is an evolving journey. Making curriculum plans that enhanced learning for special children whetted my appetite to explore many avenues of research, especially in science and social studies.

The journey from Christian education back into secular education can be pinpointed more precisely. To fulfill a requirement of the Baptist Foreign Mission Board and to pay back a loan, I began teaching public school between my college and seminary years. So positive was that experience that I was never able to shove it aside.

Those two years of teaching after obtaining my seminary degree, coupled with unlimited opportunities for leadership roles in my church, expanded my person-hood. My commitment to public education was so strong, my marriage later on included the promise I would someday return to teaching school—which I did when my son entered first grade.

Chapter 10

Catching Claude

"He surrounded me with a love and stability that had
evaded me most of my life."

Can a committee spawn a romance? The first time I met my husband-to-be was
when he came by Tattnall Square Baptist Church in Macon, Georgia, where I
worked as a Christian educator in 1958. He told me I had been assigned to his
county-wide missions committee.

He didn't stay long, but he did stay long enough to make a positive impression.
After he left I asked, "Who is that preacher and what do you know about him?"

"He's Claude Mason," said one of the secretaries, "and he's the pastor of
Second Baptist Church."

Another added, "He lost his wife to cancer six months ago and he has a
twelve-year-old son."

For once I kept my opinions to myself. I thought, "This fellow is witty,
knowledgeable, and very handsome." The missions committee never met, but I got
a husband out of the assignment.

I made the next move. The church where I served as minister of education was
located on the campus of Mercer University. Consequently, I did a lot of work with
college students.

Plans for a college retreat were in the making. Everything was complete except
for a campfire speaker, so I called Claude and he agreed to come. Max, his twelve-
year-old son, also came.

A month passed and I heard nothing from Claude. My church sponsored
a statewide mission conference and he attended. After the rally Claude took a
missionary friend of mine from our college days together, Helen Holmes Ruchti,
and me out for dinner. During the course of our table conversation, Claude
mentioned his wife had recently died of cancer.

My friend, Helen, expressed her regrets, but I'm not sure what I mouthed. Thanks to my church staff, I already knew about his wife. Soon we shifted the conversation back to the living. How stupid of me, thinking I could stifle his anguish simply by ignoring it.

Time passed and my phone was silent. Then one day Claude called and asked me to accompany him to a church where he was holding revival services. For those unfamiliar, a revival is the time when a preacher tries to get the church membership to do what they should have been doing all along. I went.

That night Claude, with animation, preached about Ahab and Jezebel. When we returned to my apartment, he kissed me goodnight. He mentioned several attempts his preacher friends and church members had made to match him up with someone. I didn't fully understand at the time what he meant when he said, "I feel more alive tonight than I have since my wife passed away."

Soon we became a steady twosome. On our dates we went bowling or played miniature golf. Knowing Claude was a consummate fisherman, I would not shut up until he agreed to take me fishing. Once was enough. All those squiggly worms and slimy fish—I could not wait to get home and take a hot bath.

On one of our dates Claude said, "You'd better seriously consider our age difference."

"How old are you?" I asked.

"Eighteen years older than you. It may not matter now, but there may come a time when it will."

I knew he was older than I was. But it was hard for me to fathom a difference of eighteen years. Besides, I was in love and the years would have to be dealt with in due time.

I had already alerted him to the emotional problems in my family, allowing him to read the life history I had earlier prepared for our denomination's missions board. He took my past in stride.

The common thread that brought and held us together was our vocational callings. His was to preach, mine to teach. Both of us could well be described as workaholics. I was more addicted than Claude. He rarely missed taking a day off each week to go fishing.

While our "callings" cemented our relationship, we had a lot of differences. Claude liked to fish; I liked to read. He seldom met a stranger; I did not open up until I got to know a person well. I enjoyed all phases of the arts, especially drama; Claude's interest in plays paralleled my interest in fishing.

The only fish I was interested in hauling in was Claude Mason. In that regard I landed the big one.

I had lots of experience teaching twelve-year-olds. But was I ready to become a mother to one? Prior to our engagement, Claude arranged for Max and me to meet. I wasn't expecting what I got.

42

Max was large for his age both in weight and in height. Barefooted and clad in pedal pushers he raced to the car and shouted, "Shot gun!"—meaning he had access to the outside seat.

When we got to the diner he ordered a double cheeseburger, a large order of fries, and a super-sized Coke. For the next thirty minutes he buried his head in a comic book. I realized this wasn't getting the results we wanted. Finally his father interceded and we had a fairly good conversation. We developed common interests around bowling and comedy and sports television programs.

Claude and I made plans for a December 7, 1959 wedding. The church where I served as minister of education and the one where my husband-to-be was pastor both felt they should host the wedding. So I solved that problem by opting to have the wedding in my home church in Savannah.

I botched some things early on. We'd been married less than three months when a member of his church, a young policeman, died of a heart attack. Claude was overcome with grief. I couldn't decipher whether he was grieving for the young man in question or whether he was reliving his grief over the death of his first wife.

I wrongly interpreted it to mean he no longer loved me. I now know both of his emotions were natural, acceptable responses and totally unrelated to his love for me.

Despite my lack of domestic skills, I zestfully took in stride being a newlywed, a preacher's wife, and a mother to a twelve-year-old boy.

We had been married only a couple of months when I received some startling news. For weeks I'd been busy making preparations to teach a group of adults in a citywide project. On the night of that special event I had a strange, eerie feeling. I felt weaker than warmed-over dishwater and soon broke out in a rash.

The next morning I wasted no time getting to our family doctor. My self-diagnosis was that I had been hit with a flu bug. The doctor did some preliminary checking and then told me to have a seat.

"Lynelle," he said, "you don't have the flu. You're pregnant."

"What? Are you sure?" I asked.

"Yes, I'm sure. Does that bother you?"

"Oh, no," I answered. "A baby was always in our long range plans. But, gee, whiz, I've only been married two months."

"That's long enough," said the doctor, chuckling. "Let me see you again in a month."

The months passed slowly, but finally the big day arrived.

"Mrs. Mason, are you ready to see your baby?" asked the night nurse.

"Yes, I am," I answered with enthusiasm.

"Read me the numbers on your arm," added the nurse.

I glanced at my arm and read off a series of numbers. The nurse laughed, saying, "You got most of them. I guess it's safe to bring him in."

43

In a few minutes my baby boy lay cuddled in my arms. Instinctively, I checked his fingers and toes. My heart sang for joy as I held him close.

"Hello, baby," I cooed. "I'm your mama and I love you very, very much."

I gave him a few sips of juice and then before I knew it, the nurse was whisking him away.

I had earlier committed myself to attend an out-of-town missions conference with a group of women from our church. Three weeks later it was decision time. Claude and I discussed the pros and cons.

"Don't you understand?" I asked. "I don't want to leave my baby."

"Yes, I understand," said Claude as he gave me a quick hug. "But the trip will do you good. Besides, you'll only be gone one night."

That's true," I said, half laughing, half crying. "However, you're overlooking one little tidbit. I don't want to go!"

I lost that argument only to spend the next twenty-four hours in abject misery. The women sympathized with my plight, but even that didn't cure my malady.

As we motored home, my cure was just around the corner. Edna, our baby-sitter and friend, answered the doorbell with Alan in her arms. Upon hearing my voice, Alan leaped—as if he'd found someone he'd been searching for. Edna was the first to notice his deliberate response. As for me, I went into orbit. What a welcome home!

From day one Claude measured up. I could not have asked for a more loving, caring partner. He was there for me during my pregnancy and at the time of Alan's birth. He took the midnight shift for bottle duty. And as Alan grew older, Claude rode the rims off the stroller giving his son rides up and down the avenue.

Reflection tells me that Claude's greatest gift to me was freeing me to find and be myself. He surrounded me with a love and stability that had evaded me most of my life. We merged our talents and centered our love in our home and church.

Claude was proud of my skills as a minister of education and encouraged me to use them. Later when I resumed my work as a public school teacher, he was my number-one cheerleader.

Both of us were committed to following Jesus.

Lynelle and Claude on their wedding day

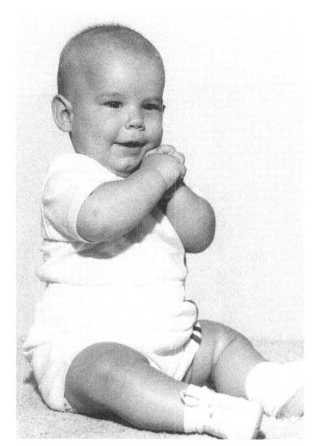

The gift of Alan

Chapter 11

A New Place

"I had a lot to learn."

A committee brought Claude and me together. A committee would lead our family to a new place to call home. Committees seem to have a big impact on Baptists.

Slightly before our second wedding anniversary a pulpit committee arrived one Sunday at the Second Baptist Church of Macon, Georgia. When a pulpit committee visits a Baptist church they create quite a stir. Immediately upon their arrival the regular members start nudging one another and swapping knowing looks.

Rossville First Baptist Church, located in the northwestern corner of Georgia, was without a pastor and the search committee came to hear Claude. When the service was over, the committee members invited us to lunch. After talking for some time, we were ready for step two: we would visit their church and Claude would preach a trial sermon.

One aspect of that visit is very revealing about Claude. Even after he committed himself to become their pastor, he still did not know what his salary would be. In the realm of preachers, that is indeed a rarity.

My first impression of the little mill town of Rossville in 1961 wasn't favorable. My complaint? Most of the women in the local restaurant wore blue jeans. Of course they wore blue jeans; they were on their way to work at the local mill! I had a lot to learn.

Most churches of any denomination with a "first" attached to their name have a position of respect and leadership within their community. Generally speaking, in a First Baptist congregation there will be more people with college degrees and more who are engaged in professional fields of work.

I secretly harbored hopes that by becoming the pastor of the First Baptist Church, my husband would have the prestige I felt he deserved. I vainly thought my talents would be appreciated and used as well.

At any rate, we said our goodbyes to the Macon congregation and headed to the beautiful hills of Northwest Georgia. Rossville, our new location, is a small town on the state border leading into Chattanooga, Tennessee.

Chattanooga, like Savannah at the time, still clung to its downtown department stores, mainly Loveman's and Miller Brothers. All the motion picture shows were downtown, too.

Alan was unaware of the move, but at age thirteen, Max was convinced his life lay in ruins. He was enjoying the status of puppy love, and now all of that had come to a screeching halt. He wept all the way from Macon to Rossville.

Alan, just three days away from his first birthday, was quiet and content in his mama's lap, constantly trying to remove my glasses and squealing "cockes"—his baby talk version for glasses.

Before we got unpacked, two of our neighbor's teenage sons began circling around our house. Soon they knocked on our door and introduced themselves.

They made friends with Max and just like a touch of magic, his tears disappeared. Max made a total about-face when he learned the Rossville High School Bulldogs were contenders for the Georgia state football championship.

Chapter 12

Great Expectations

"At times I felt like I was walking a tight wire in a circus."

In 1966 I went back to teaching when Alan entered the first grade. Being a wife, mother, church worker, and third grade teacher didn't leave me any "goof-off" time. At times I felt like I was walking a tight wire in a circus.

Although I had a master's degree in religious education, the state of Georgia put me on a provisional certificate and a substandard pay scale. The first education course I took for full certification was in teaching "new math."

In the end I got an "A" in the course, but between the beginning and end I nearly went nuts trying to do simple addition, subtraction, multiplication, and division from a base system other than our usual base ten. The algorithms that were supposed to make it easier for children to learn math dumbfounded me. Suffice it to say that this "new math" never endured in Georgia, or for that matter, in any state.

At church I switched from being the unpaid youth director to working with children ages nine through twelve.

Fortunately, Alan and I gradually became acclimated to our new school environments. Alan went on to become a star pupil, and I found myself wondering how I could beg or borrow enough time to do all I needed to do with my third graders.

After school each day, as I graded papers and made lesson plans, Alan visited with others on our school staff. One of his all-time favorites was a fifth grade teacher. One day she told him about one of her pupils throwing a temper tantrum that morning. Alan's cagey six-year-old response was, "I've learned that doesn't work at my house."

One afternoon when he was six, Alan, his best friend, and I were talking as usual. The steeple on our new sanctuary had been hoisted that morning.

"Who is in charge of our church?" I asked.

His friend spoke up saying, "Brother Mason."

"And Alan," I asked, "who do you think is in charge?"

"Jesus is in charge," he said, "and Daddy is his helper."

I hid his response in the pocket of my heart, knowing his faith years were light years ahead of his chronological age.

That same summer he nestled up in his daddy's lap and said, "Daddy, we need to talk."

"O.K., Sport, what's on your mind?"

"I think you'll want to turn off the television and get your Bible."

His dad smiled and said, "Let's go to my bedroom. It's quiet there."

When they got settled in, Alan said, "Daddy, I want to become a Christian."

"That's good. Let's talk about it."

I waited in an adjoining bedroom until Claude called me to join them. The three of us, through tears, thanked God for Alan's decision. I remember thinking, God has something very special in mind for Alan and somehow I'm going to be a part of it.

The following Sunday, Alan went forward at the close of the church service making his decision known to the entire congregation, as is the custom in Baptist churches.

Alan loved music. In the second grade he began taking piano lessons and did so through his undergraduate years in college.

A professional friend of mine, in an adjoining county, that same year loaned me an intelligence test that supposedly took ten minutes to give and would, in return, give the teacher a fair indicator of a child's mental age.

Alan became my first case study. I corralled him one Saturday night and started popping questions. The test was set up so that the test administrator would quit asking questions when a child missed ten questions in a row. Alan readily got to the place where he'd miss one or two questions out of ten, and then it went to five or six.

One hour later I was still asking him questions. I calculated the results and thought maybe I had done something wrong. His I.Q. was very high.

Soon it was time for Alan to enter the third grade, and I was faced with an embarrassing problem. Our principal had a weird way of assigning pupils. Final classroom rolls were made during the summer. However, if parents wanted their children to be in a particular teacher's room the following year, the request had to be made during the last week of school.

All of Alan's classmates were enrolling in my class. Since I had no intention of being Alan's teacher, this presented me with a unique problem. So I offered to take all the children with academic or social problems so that Alan's class could move up intact.

The years rolled by and Alan, when eleven, made the switch from elementary to junior high without a bobble. Now forty years old, I paid no attention to his first slight of me. But when it happened again and again, I took notice. He needed breathing room from me, and I reluctantly concurred.

It took some adjusting for me to move from top billing. I finally caught on that his distancing himself was mostly window dressing for his peers. While he was in the seventh grade he became a member of the high school band program. Alan played the clarinet during the marching season and the oboe for concert performances.

"Oboe?" I asked. "I've never heard of that instrument. Why did you choose the oboe?"

"Because it's one of the hardest instruments to play," he replied.

"What makes it so hard to play?"

"The sound comes through a thin reed, and you must have good breath control."

Alan was setting his own agenda. So, why was I uneasy?

Chapter 13

A Road Less Traveled

"I sat there trying to project myself into the future …
and became enmeshed in a sea of 'what ifs.'"

There was only one other young child in our subdivision when we moved to Rossville. She was two years older than Alan and lived across the street from us.

His little friend often brought her doll when she came to our house. When he was two years old Alan wanted a doll, too. So I bought him a boy doll and dressed it in overalls.

At other times when he and I would act out Cinderella, his favorite fairy tale, he always wanted to be Cinderella and I kept insisting he be Prince Charming. I seldom won. Our church pianist gave him an old skirt, and he loved to put it on and do a commercial ditty of the sixties called "The Pineapple Twist."

The girls who came to the church nursery were avid Barbie and Ken collectors. Alan readily joined their ranks. Did it ever occur to me that his preschool choices were unusual? Yes. Did I consider his actions to be different? The answer to that is both yes and no.

However, armed with Doctor Spock's sage advice, I let myself become convinced he was merely a preschooler engaging in creative play. For every unusual behavior he showed, I could list a complementing behavior he practiced that was normal for any child. One thing was obvious: Alan was not a "guns and guts" kind of boy.

I can't remember a time when Alan didn't enjoy the world of books.

"Alan," I'd say, "get a few books and we'll read."

He'd spin around, and by the time I looked down he was climbing onto my lap laden with books. He was still hooked on his pacifier and in diapers when we first visited the public library in our little town.

Alan's love for books was only rivaled by his love of music. I bought a series of Walt Disney stories and movie recordings for his first birthday. It became one of the best investments of my life.

When it came to disciplining Alan, a good firm "no" worked most of the time. There was one notable exception. I had a stereo, a prized possession, left over from my single days. After observing me work the machine a time or two, Alan decided he could do it without my help.

When things got too quiet around our house, I knew where to go looking. He either would be trying to operate the stereo or the "on" button on our black-and-white television. We took the control knobs off the television and replaced them with a pair of pliers. But the stereo didn't fare so well. After several months of "Alan abuse," it was never again usable.

During Alan's pre-kindergarten days we went as a family to support our Rossville Bulldogs football team. Alan, now three, was satisfied through halftime. However, after the band performed he'd become so sleepy that we would have to go home.

Once at home he'd put on Sousa's "Stars and Stripes Forever." Then he'd march up and down our huge living room until I thought his tiny legs would drop off. Since I have a long history of singing off tune, I was delighted to have a son enmeshed in musical adventures.

Alan once pinned a clothespin on the tail of his kitten, and thanks to Mary Poppins drew pictures with colored chalk on the hardwood floor of his bedroom, and wore out several umbrellas trying to fly. Alan was lazy about picking up his toys and had a cunning habit of getting everything to come out in his favor. He didn't pout, sulk, or throw temper tantrums. Nevertheless, he managed to get his way.

Alan went to kindergarten in 1965 when he was four, and everything went well except for one minor mishap. One day he brought home a painting that resembled a thunderstorm. After a little probing I discovered it was supposed to be a rural farm scene. Okay, I thought, so my son isn't going to be the world's next Picasso.

Secretly the excessive overlap of black markings bothered me. This continued for two more days before I talked with his teacher. The only thing that had changed, she noted, was his reading schedule. She sensed Alan was far more interested in reading than in drawing pictures. She moved Alan in with the older children, and then there were no more dark and stormy pictures.

The year ended and a new one began. I was thirty-six in 1966. Alan and I were two weeks into the new school year, and we were both doing tailspins. I'd agreed to teach the third grade, a grade I'd never taught. I read and re-read my teacher's guidebooks.

"How will I stretch this meager bit of material over nine months?" I pondered.

More than two-thirds of my pupils were from the church my husband served as pastor. One day as I was verbalizing some yearly goals, a little blond cherub, from a prominent church family, burst into tears. "What's wrong?" I asked.

"I'll never be able to do all of that!" she said, trying to mute her sobs. Concurrently another pupil got the stomachache every day when we started to do our reading workbooks.

While all of this was happening to me, Alan was making mad dashes back to the car every morning, begging his dad to take him home.

In those days our school system had a Bible teacher who came once a week. And in addition to their storytelling, teachers were given a Bible verse for each child to learn.

In Alan's class, taught by a graduate of Bob Jones University, the children got an "A" only if they had their verse memorized by Monday. Nothing was mentioned about the verse until Alan hopped into bed on Sunday night. All of a sudden he began crying.

What's wrong?" I asked.

"My Bible verse," he said between sobs. "I forgot to learn it."

"That's okay. We'll work on it tomorrow."

"No, Mama, that won't do. I have to know it tomorrow or I won't get an 'A.'"

I didn't do a very good job of concealing my fury over my son getting a grade in Bible. I knew the verse he was to learn because it was the same as the one for my third graders. I cuddled him in my arms, and we went over the short verse until he could say it smoothly. He went to sleep, but I stayed awake rethinking the pitfalls of teaching the Bible in our public schools.

At the end of Alan's first six weeks in the first grade, his teacher and I went over the results of the battery of tests that he and his classmates had taken. He had done extremely well in all of his academic subjects. Then she showed me a picture Alan had drawn of himself.

It was a stick figure wearing a skirt. With my tunnel vision in full play I dismissed it as meaningless—sort of.

My son wasn't fitting into the norm, and it bothered me. It was a "black night of the soul" moment that gripped me, refusing to let go.

One Saturday I sat alone in the den. Alan and his dad were in another room watching a basketball game on television. Alan was jumping up and down, doing flips and repeating chants to cheer his team to victory.

It hit me like a bolt of lightning. If Alan is gay, what will I do? Will I be non-accepting and deny the child of my womb, the light of my life? Will I excuse his behavior and jeopardize my relationship with my heavenly father?

At this point in time I saw sexual orientation in shades of black and white.

"Oh, God," I prayed, "Please don't test me as you did Abraham. Don't make me choose between you and my son."

I sighed a primeval sigh, then continued, "If choose I must, then I'll go with you. For you alone are Lord of my life."

No sooner had I uttered those words than I knew in my heart of hearts that I questioned them.

I sat there trying to project myself into the future when Alan would be a young adult, and I became enmeshed in a sea of "what ifs." The imagining was gut wrenching.

Once again my mind returned to my brother John, who spent most of his adult life in and out of mental institutions. What kind of demon lurked around the corner, ready to devour my son?

Ultimately I concluded that all my thoughts were much ado about nothing. After all, Alan was a model child, an excellent student, and related well with adults and his peers of both sexes.

"Oh, God," I prayed, "If I have failed at being a good mother, then I am a total, miserable failure. Have mercy on me."

Soon it was time for supper so I got busy in the kitchen, keeping my disturbing thoughts to myself. What made me wonder about Alan's sexual orientation at this specific time? After all, he had not done anything overtly that warranted my concern.

Perhaps it was the testosterone urge running rampant among his peers at church. Boys and girls were forming liaisons, sitting in church together, and incessantly passing notes during church services. Although Alan was a favorite with many of the girls, he showed no signs of preteen infatuation.

Memories of teaching the seventh grade for a year were still vivid in my mind. The lack of building funds in 1957 caused the seventh graders to be temporarily housed in the elementary school.

I should have known better. But I was young and naïve. Teaching sixth graders had been a delightful experience. So, what did I do? I volunteered to go up with my class and be their seventh grade teacher.

Teacher textbooks talk about it, but I was to get my education in the raw. Nothing I had ever read could have prepared me for the changes I saw when my sixth graders returned as seventh graders in September.

Formerly studious, polite girls became constant gigglers and busy note writers/passers. The boys spent their time answering notes and discussing sports. Alan was not going through this change.

By now it was clear Alan was choosing a road less traveled. He demanded excellence from himself and got it. Alan was the kind of student every teacher dreamed of getting but seldom got.

There were no blatant sexual reasons for me to consider him gay. Different? Yes. Gifted and goal oriented? Yes.

At home Alan was loving and respectful. At church he was active in the youth music program, being the pianist for the youth choir.

Early on, Alan won the heart of his seventh-grade music teacher. He became her student aide and had a piano solo in every program she put together for the school.

One night, toward the close of the seventh grade, Alan and I were alone in the den. "Mom," he said, "I've a problem and I need help."

"Yes," I said, "go on."

"Some of the guys at school are telling everyone I'm gay."

"What do you think it means to be gay?"

"You know, when guys like other guys instead of liking girls."

I waited.

"It isn't true," he said, "I'm not gay and it makes me mad to hear them talk that way."

"Why don't you talk it over with one of your male teachers? They'll give you some good suggestions as to how to stop it. Or, if you like, we can go see a counselor."

"I'll talk with my homeroom teacher. I feel close to him. Thanks, Mom."

In a week or so the name-calling ceased. And me? I preferred to believe it was much ado about nothing.

Alan's teen years were rather placid. He spent most of his time studying and practicing the piano, clarinet, and oboe. "Squeak, squeak, squeak!" went the noise emanating from his bedroom. On and on he'd go. Day after day came forth the same squeak, squeak, squeaks.

How on earth, I thought, can those gosh-awful sounds ever turn into music? I found myself moving to other parts of the house to keep from listening.

A lot of things happened, some good and some bad, when Alan was in the eighth grade. Max, my stepson returned from Vietnam and with his bride, Donna, moved to Atlanta to enroll in pharmacy school. Soon they had a baby boy, Patrick Ross, making me a grandmother at thirty-nine and Alan an uncle at thirteen.

Alan adapted to his new role better than I, for I felt awkward having a grand-son while being the mother of a teenage son.

Chapter 14

Tempest in the Fish Bowl

"I wish we had made more time for one another."

The pastor search committee in Rossville had been impressed with my credentials as well as Claude's. It never entered my mind to stand on the sidelines and serve in some bland traditional mold. I found our church hungry for leadership in the field of religious education, so lost little time in bringing it assistance.

I felt as if all of my training and service were in demand. Early on we began to have overnight retreats, socials, and plays that called out skills from our youth. At the same time I became the teacher of the girls youth class and soon became the Sunday evening Church Training leader of the youth group that included girls and boys.

In less than a year we had an active youth council with a gutsy calendar of activities. I was greatly assisted by Ann McDaniel, who shared her remarkable skills with all of us. Banquets were her specialty. We managed to spring a banquet for every holiday.

Sponsoring the annual Youth Week was one of my specialties. Both the youth and adults thought well of this venture.

Well before the youth work became established, Edna Ruth Mavity and Betty Astin sought my assistance with the girls in our missions organization. Readily I recalled the impact such an organization had on my life during my teen years. How could I refuse?

While the list of service requirements was daunting, our young women arose to the challenge. Soon, our church crowned Sandra (Sandy) Swafford as Queen-with-a-Scepter, the highest honor Southern Baptists bestowed on girls. For years to come, we had coronation services for new queens.

I became an active part of the Woman's Missionary Union. Pleasant vibes still linger of the dinner roll contests between May Ferguson and Lucy Stonecipher. The Mason family could have cared less. We gladly took what was left over from both of them.

Where was my child during this hubbub of activities? Alan attended many of the activities and when that wasn't feasible, there was always Miss Joy. The wife of a retired Navy officer, Miss Joy and Alan quickly bonded. She was loving, firm, and creative. I thank God for her enriching ministry to all the children of First Baptist.

Claude and I had settled into our marriage too quickly, acting like a couple who had been married ten years instead of two. I'm not sure whom to fault. Probably both of us bear blame.

I became engrossed in being a mother while Claude found his pastoral duties invigorating. To complicate matters, our church had some kind of meeting going on every night of the week. I attended many of the meetings, and Claude attended all of them. I wish we had made more time for one another.

My husband and I were both committed to helping our church grow. However, for Claude the people of our congregation got top billing. Almost every vacation we took was cut short by a phone call, asking him to return for a funeral. There was no need to talk it over. We always came home.

Our aborted vacations included trips to Florida, Virginia, Washington, D.C., New York City, and the Bahama Islands. Meeting the needs of our church family was held in greater esteem than our personal needs.

Spending the night in a hospital was a big deal for me, even if it was considered minor surgery. Claude left me to preach a funeral in Alabama. That hurt.

I soon found being married to a preacher akin to living in a fish bowl. What I said, wore, and did became fodder for the church gossips. I was determined to live by my own standards, even if it produced ruffled feathers. I even expressed my views on the hot topic of the sixties: racial integration.

The thing that kept me out of trouble was that on subjects where I knew there were strong differences I always labeled my opinion as my own, allowing those who disagreed the same privilege. Besides, most of them approved of my work with their youth and children. It's hard for parents to fault someone their children adore.

Fast-forwarding this story, the golden years of our ministry at First Baptist Church of Rossville began in 1970 and ended in1978.

A vacancy on our church staff led to an interview with Bill Hix for the position of minister of music and youth. Soon Bill and Janice Hix were at work. At the height of their ministry among us, the ranks of our youth choir grew to fifty. The youth choir produced excellent musical dramas, went on extended trips, and swelled our Sunday evening attendance records.

While Bill and Janice were the creative instigators and sustainers of the youth choir, they were assisted by many lay helpers. Claude bonded readily with the youth and was their number-one fan and supporter. Harriett Michaels saw that the youth were fed every Sunday. She kept this position for eight years, and I can't remember an occasion when she faltered.

During the time our youth movement was growing by leaps and bounds, I was deeply involved in my duties as a public school teacher. My church activities became limited. We had a small but active group of women who didn't consider ourselves old enough to be in a senior Bible study class. We called ourselves young adults, but that was perhaps begging the question. One thing is certain: The friendship ties nurtured in that group of about fifteen women are still generating hope and love today.

Yet, unknown to me at the time, a royal battle was brewing in the music ministry of our church. As the story came to me, it was over what the adult choir would sing for Easter. They openly rejected Bill's selection.

Following this conflict, Bill and Jan decided it was time for them to leave. They had no problem finding a home at Ozark Baptist Church in Ozark, Alabama, where they remained for the next thirty years until retirement. However, their departure signaled the beginning of the end of numerical growth and spiritual harmony at First Baptist.

Claude was still grieving over the abrupt departure of Bill, Jan, and their son, Michael (who had become like a grandson to him) when he and a senior deacon were asked to seek a new minister of music and youth. They asked a young man and his wife from New Orleans Baptist Seminary to come for an interview.

This had to be the biggest misjudgment Claude ever made in his long, successful career. It was like turning loose a bevy of angry bees in close proximity. What evolved was a clash between what was then considered classic Southern Baptist protocol and charismatic innovations. In a matter of months the situation became worse and wound up with the church terminating the music minister's services. There was enough blame for everyone to share in this chapter of our church history. Several families left the church, and Claude began planning for his retirement.

Every church has at least one troublemaker. Our church was no exception.

Jill, who was in her late forties, had been married twice, sang in the adult choir, taught adults in Sunday school, and held a responsible position at a local bank. She had been suspect on my list long before she became chief troublemaker of the adult choir.

I didn't know about her musical talents, but I knew her interpretation of Scripture was vastly different from mine. Jill spoke of having visions, spouted her opinions as facts, and felt our church was woefully unspiritual. She connoted spirituality with frequent shouts of "Amen" and following unstructured forms of worship. I was always uncomfortable in Jill's presence.

Claude was depressed and secretly angry when Barry came for a trial visit and interview. We should have taken it as a bad omen when Jill and her followers enthusiastically latched on to Barry, but we didn't.

Barry was charismatic and emotional. He soon ignored Claude and began taking orders from Jill, thinking she was the secret to his success. It did not take long until Claude and I both knew the church had a bad worm, perhaps several bad worms. One morning I counted Barry's shouted "Amens!" until they reached forty and then, in disgust, quit counting.

Our church members were fuming and fussing, and some I suspect were cussing. Eighteen years of love and ministry were being threatened. It became certain that Claude would resign and Barry would take over, or we would stay and Barry would resign. Jill spearheaded the group backing Barry.

Most Baptist business meetings are the epitome of dullsville. Reports are given and accepted, and recommendations, if there are any, are addressed. Then we sing a hymn, have a prayer, and go home. But when the deacons called for Barry's resignation, all hell broke loose.

For starters the church was packed. Even those without an opinion were there to watch the fur fly. After the motion to have Barry resign was made, the floor was opened for discussion. Tempers flared and passionate pleas and accusations filled the air. However, in the end, reason prevailed and the motion was passed.

From Texas, while a student at Baylor University, Alan wrote:

Mom and Dad,

You are both in my prayers along with First Baptist Church. Mrs. Flint's poem, "What God Hath Promised," helped me when I was blue about the week you all had. I hope her message means as much to you as it did to me.

God hath not promised
Skies always blue,
Flower-strewn pathways
All our lives through;
God hath not promised
Sun without rain,
Joy without sorrow,
Peace without pain.

But God hath promised
Strength for the day,
Rest for the labor,
Light for the way,
Grace for trials,
Help from above,
Unfailing sympathy,
Undying love.

To my biggest fans and, most importantly, best friends, I can only say you are what you should be! I've never doubted it. I love you.

Alan

You would think that the church's action would have been the end of the matter, but it wasn't. Jill had been crossed, and she wasn't about to take the dismissal of Barry without a fight. She began pushing, behind the scenes, for Claude to resign. She did not succeed, but she was influential, I think, in his retiring earlier than he had planned.

Perhaps a temperament explanation is in order. It was easy for me to get angry, to speak my mind, and move on. Claude, on the other hand, had worked his entire life on controlling his temper. Whenever I'd want to argue, he'd leave the room or take a walk outside and leave me to stew in my own juices. When something big bothered him, he internalized his hurts and went on with his business as if nothing had happened.

I was mad enough to explode. Once matters had come to a head concerning Bill and Jan, there had been one small church skirmish after another. We were a divided people. Everyone seemed out of joint. Even people we considered to be lifetime friends became distant. Like a pot of boiling water, Claude's anger simmered against Jill. But still he said nothing.

One night it hit an all-time low.

I was sitting in the den when the phone rang. "Hello," I said.

In a whispery voice Jill said, "I want to ask you a question. You can just answer yes or no if Claude is nearby."

"What is it you want to ask?"

"Are you planning to divorce Claude?"

"Why should I?"

"Somebody told me you were."

"Listen," I said, "I don't appreciate your phone call. First of all, it isn't any of your business. But since you asked, the answer is no."

Without further ado I hung up the phone and went and told Claude.

The next day Claude's simmering pot of emotions erupted. He stormed into the bank where Jill worked, demanding to speak to her. For thirty minutes they had an angry exchange.

I knew it would never do for me to stand up and tell our people how I really felt. Preachers' wives aren't accorded that liberty. So, what did I do? I wrote about my feelings and felt justified when it came out in a Southern Baptist Convention drama publication, three years prior to the time the convention would take a big turn toward the religious right.

There were no winners. Jill lost. Claude lost. Our fractured church became the

63

biggest loser. Jill and her disgruntled cronies left the church. Two years later Claude would retire.

The deacons stipulated two final requests from Claude. The first was that he head up a fund to build a new fellowship hall and secondly that he and a committee of deacons seek out a new music and youth minister. Claude readily accepted their requests. It was easy raising the money for the much-needed fellowship hall. Soon, David Helms, a recent graduate of Southern Seminary, accepted the call to become our music and youth minister, even though he knew Claude's retirement was imminent. Under the leadership of David and Carolyn Helms, both the adult and youth choirs prospered.

Before our departure the church made Claude pastor emeritus and feted us with a great celebration party that drew a host of people from far and near. At this time I was at the height of my teaching career and Alan was completing his freshman year at Baylor University.

The final years of Claude's life found us very close. He backed all my teaching innovations with special children and my new love for creative writing. He became my encourager and number-one fan. My retirement from teaching gave me a special year to devote to Claude's escalating bout with heart problems. When it counted most we were there for one another.

Chapter 15

Big Adventures

"God sure was getting my requests all mixed up lately."

Professionally, I had entered a new educational field called learning disabilities. My work was rewarding, intriguing, demanding, and sometimes confusing.

Alan had taken well to Baylor University. He had great grades and was involved with youth projects at his college church.

While in high school he had received catalogs from several Baptist schools. Only Furman and Baylor offered degrees in oboe performance. We discovered that our neighbor's sister taught oboe at Baylor University. Soon, Alan was getting mail and phone calls from her and others in Waco, Texas.

When it came time for him to move a thousand miles from home, we decided his dad would accompany Alan to Waco. Claude could help him get settled in, leave the car with Alan, and then fly home.

Deep inside I knew this was far more than a casual trip. Nothing would ever be the same again. After all, I mused to myself, that's what college is all about.

Why was cutting the apron strings so hard? I wanted to let go, and yet I didn't want to let go. On Sunday morning before he left for Baylor, Alan played the postlude on the church organ. Uncontrolled tears gushed down my face like a cascading waterfall. There, in plain view of our entire church family, I burst into crocodile-size tears.

After settling into college life, Alan wrote:

Mom and Dad,

Good to talk with you, Mom. Sorry I missed talking with you, Dad. I am having a wonderful time making friends, studying, going on retreats, and worshiping. I love you both and am praying

for you each day. Pray that God might use my life the way he sees
fit. I know he led me to Baylor for a reason, and I am going to
search until I find that purpose.

   P.S. Mom, don't worry about new Church Training ideas. I
have experienced enough for two people in these first two weeks. I'll
let you know about some of them soon.

When Alan was home for the summer after his sophomore year, he hinted there might be something he was withholding from me.

As was my custom, I always stayed awake reading until he came in. He slipped into the bedroom, gave me a good night kiss, and said, "I'm so afraid someday I'll do something that will disappoint you. I love you, Mom."

I quickly hushed such talk, saying, "I can't imagine any direction you could ever take that would separate the two of us."

Nevertheless, sleep for me that night was gone and his words kept returning again and again in my dream thoughts.

Then the summer after his junior year at college Alan told me, "There are some things I will keep as a secret forever."

Is he trying to tell me he's gay? I wondered.

I decided not to probe but to wait, believing that if he were gay, in due time he'd tell me his secret. Meanwhile, I revved up my prayer life, continually asking God for some girl to come along and win his heart.

When Alan neared graduation from Baylor, there was never a question as to whether he would attend graduate school. However, he wanted some time to regroup and to explore his options. This led him to apply to become a "journeyman"—a two-year assignment from the Southern Baptist Convention's world missions program.

One day he called and told me: "Mom, guess what? The mission board accepted me." He hesitated and then asked, "Are you sitting down?"

"Yes," I added, "where are they sending you?"

"Senegal, West Africa. I'll teach English to the people who come to the International Center."

I mumbled, "Did I hear you right? Did you say Africa?"

My mind exploded with visions of boa constrictors, sweltering heat, life-threatening diseases, and huge sand dunes. "Aren't there any alternatives?" I asked.

"Mom, you don't understand. I want to go to Africa. In Senegal I'll get to use French and learn Wolof, their tribal language."

Alan wrote from Texas:

Mom and Dad,

*You have given me more than I can begin to repay. You taught
me by your lives grace, forgiveness, acceptance, freedom, and love.
When I am at my lowest I know that there are least two people in
the world who love me. I live off that security. You also led me to
the source of your love for others and me: Jesus Christ. That gift
exceeds everything. It is the gift of hope, the dawning of a new
Alan, the Alan that God is shaping into a Light. You led me to God
by being authentic Christians. You talked of sharing and shared.
You talked of dedication and faith, and I watched you stay beyond
a reasonable time at Rossville First Baptist just because you believed
that faith must have feet. You've given me a glimpse of Christ's face.
Wherever I go, whatever I become, I know my faith will accompany me, guiding and illuminating the way. But it doesn't lessen
the intensity of the confusion and struggle. Pray with me for direction in my life. Again, and put more simply, I love you. I miss your
faces, eyes, voices. But we will be together again. Physical distance
can never separate us.*

Alan

No parent was ever more thrilled that her son had chosen to serve as a
missionary overseas for two years. But Africa was another story. God sure was
getting my requests all mixed up lately.

Alan came home for two weeks before leaving for journeyman training.
During this time, Jan, a friend from his university, came for a four-day visit. Was
she a future wife prospect? It was obvious she thought so, but I wasn't so sure.

After Alan left for journeyman orientation in North Carolina, I found a
scribbled note that read:

*Last night I dreamed I was a child again running and playing on
Sunset Drive. I was hunting desperately for something I had lost. I
woke up before I found it.*

What did this note mean? Then, dated 8-1-83, we received the following fax gram:

I arrived safely. Love, Alan

Meanwhile, we talked every Saturday by phone, provided the telephone lines were
working in Dakar, the capital city of Senegal, West Africa. Three months elapsed
before Alan composed his first newsletter:

Dear Friends,

There is no way I can summarize all I've experienced the first three months of my stay in Dakar. So I have chosen instead to relate some of the sights that have opened my eyes in hope you might share in something of their meaning to me.

I shall certainly never forget my arrival at Yoff International Airport. It was a sweltering African Sunday morning, and of course the terminal was not air-conditioned. I was hot and tired from the nine-hour flight, and a little nervous. As I waited in a long line for visa clearance, I scanned the crowd who had come to greet the plane for some American faces. There were some whites, but none bore any resemblance to the photographs I had seen of my advisors, Frank and Sally Cawthon.

The plane had been late arriving, so I didn't panic. I simply told myself the missionaries, being busy sorts, had already come and would return for me before I had finished with customs. Unfortunately, I was merely deluding myself for after I picked up my bags, went through customs without a problem, and began to wait outside the airport, I realized that it was time for action. I ordered a taxi, agreeing on a price that was unreasonable (the least of my concerns at the moment), and gave the driver the only address I had in Dakar.

We drove for what seemed to be an eternity—we even took a detour through the fishing village of Ouakam before we arrived at the Baptist Mission compound. I knocked at the gate and jumped up in order to see over the tall fence, just in time to catch the startled expression of a small white-haired lady peering down at me from her second-storied apartment. She yelled down, "Who is it?" I immediately replied, "A journeyman."

She hesitated as if puzzled by this utterance, then realizing what I had said rushed to the gate to welcome me to Senegal. I shall never forget her puzzled look. I can imagine how strange I must have looked to her. After all, it isn't every day that someone comes to your gate proclaiming himself to be journeyman. She probably ran over all the possible connotations that the title evoked. Is this someone just passing through, a sort of Ulysses wandering from one strange port to another? Or does he have some purpose in being here? If so, what is it?

Her face and those questions keep returning to me. Even though it was purely chance that the cable announcing my arrival

68

never came and I ended up outside the gate peering up at her over a fence, I am thankful she called me from the beginning to search out my purpose in being here.

Another memory that continues to have meaning for me took place in a room no bigger than the average American living room. There were two hundred children, five workers, and some U.S. and African rhythm instruments. Obviously it was crowded, noisy, and very hot. Intolerable conditions I thought. It was in that place and at that time I caught a fleeting glimpse of what it means to have hope.

The children were singing, but not like what most of you call singing because they threw themselves into the act; they became the music. They were singing, "Yallah Bak Now" ("God Is So Good" in Wolof). As I surveyed the room, the irony of what they were saying slapped me across the face.

It took no keen perception to see that many of them had not eaten a good meal in weeks, that most of them had only the clothes on their backs, and that some of them were the victims of violent parents. Yet they kept on singing. These very kids, the hungry ones, the poor ones, the abused ones, were singing about God's goodness and believe it or not, my friends, they meant every bit of it. All the pain the world wrings out of them daily couldn't kill their song.

They caused me to reflect on my comfortable faith, my lack of courage, and my lack of hope. They taught me to pray that morning with the Father in the gospel of Mark: "I do believe; help my unbelief."

I can still see Babakar's face the first time I met him—goatee protruding from a pointed chin, black eyes dancing with mirth, ebony skin glistening. Introduced to me as one of only three Wolof Christians (there are 1 and 1/2 million Wolofs), I could immediately see in his face and hear in his voice the qualities which gave him the courage to be different: intelligence, wit, and honesty.

As a child he was sold by his parents to the local marabout, who in turn put Babakar on different street corners to beg for him. The marabout particularly disliked Babakar because Babakar was brave enough (or foolish enough—it's all the same, isn't it?) to confront him about the blatant differences between teachings in the Koran and his religious leader's life.

Prophets are never appreciated. Despite frequent beatings and lack of parental care, Babakar still sought out love. Luckily for him and for us, he came into contact with my advisors Sally and Frank.

He saw in their lives a connection to the New Testament that was strong and vital. As he read and studied the Bible with them, he began to see that love means more than speaking out against the bad in the world, but that real love demands creative action, which was modeled for us in the life of the one called Jesus. His frequent laughter calls me to the joyful abandonment, to truly become a "fool for Christ's sake."

"Though they may well come by accident, these moments of our seeing," writes Frederick Buechner, "I choose to believe that it is by no means by accident when they open our hearts as well as our eyes."

A cable is misplaced; someone rethinks his calling. A song is sung and the listener is challenged to hope. A goateed Wolof spins a tale of his life, and someone sees the joy of working for the coming of the Kingdom. Label them accidents or label them divine revelations: it doesn't matter. Just don't listen without opening your eyes and your heart to the world all around you.

In the Peace of Christ,
Alan Mason (alias Lamine Diope*)*

In response to receiving an article his Dad wrote titled "My Treasures," Alan wrote:

Dad, Thanks so much for your article, "My Treasures." I read it when I'm feeling bad and, although I cry because I miss you so much, I feel better when I remember I'm somebody special— your son.   *Alan*

The summer of 1984 found me, now fifty-three, in the middle of a great adventure. Alan had been in Senegal for one year and had earned seven weeks of vacation. For months he and I had been making plans to team up with Baylor University for its study/travel tour of the British Isles.

Our London base was Westminster School, adjacent to Westminster Abbey, and within a stone's throw of Parliament, Big Ben, Buckingham Palace, and the Thames River. I felt like I had stepped back into English history.

Westminster School is a public school in London, meaning it would be a private school in America. My living quarters were cramped and spartan. I slept on a cot that sank in the middle, and I had to travel down two flights of steps to get to the bath—which I'm sure was installed prior to the 1800s. Never mind the inconveniences; I was creating memories to last a lifetime.

We took in plays, symphonies, dramas, ballets, foreign films, and art museums. We drank in the scenery of Buckingham Palace, took a five-mile walking tour of Old London, made a trip to the Lake Country, visited Carnevon Castle in Wales, spent a weekend in Edinburgh, Scotland, saw some of the sights at York, and toured the House of Windsor.

Sometimes together and often separately we visited small English towns within fifty miles of London. Alan was seeing a side of me he'd never seen before. Before I knew it, we had to leave.

As the rain fell in a soft drizzle, our bus stopped long enough to give us one final view of our London home-away-from-home. For me it was a sad, tearful goodbye. To add to my frustration, one side of my eyeglasses chose at that moment to become unhinged.

We traveled across the English Channel for a three-day stay in Paris. Alan wanted to experience Paris on his own and to try out his French on the nationals. Meanwhile, I joined with other members of the tour group and went to Versailles and Chartres Cathedral.

Our last night in Paris was not a bonding time. I wrote in my journal that night:

> There goes that wall again. All I did was ask him why he didn't
> go out with the girl from Baylor who dropped by our room. There
> are times when he makes me feel cheaper than a British half-pence.
> And, to think I was stupid enough to think he would be so proud of
> the few French phrases I'd acquired before coming. He would have
> enjoyed this trip more if I hadn't come. I wished I were home.

After tossing and turning for hours I finally fell asleep. By morning the previous night was put on the back burner of my mind. Soon we would be in Africa. But before we got there, we had a major hurdle to jump.

Upon our arrival at Charles De Gaulle Airport I found a seat in the waiting room while Alan went directly to the check-in station. In a few minutes Alan rejoined me, frowning.

"What's up?" I asked.

"I forgot about the baggage load limits on Air France. My bag is way over its limit, and we can each only take on two carry-on bags."

"Come on," I said, hopping down to the carpet. "Let's open our bags. This calls for a major reshuffling."

For at least thirty minutes we sat sprawled, pulling out and swapping items. Each of us extracted a stack of books. Then Alan pulled out his sacred cache of peanut butter I had brought from Georgia.

Finally the absurdity of our situation got the best of us, and we both burst into uncontrollable giggles. My carry-on bags consisted of a basket and a flimsy shopping bag. Both were unmercifully full. We staggered like two drunks onto the plane.

Once we were seated I got my first glimpse of first-class traveling. Only a thin curtain separated us from those who dined in luxury and had someone catering to their every whim. Once again our giggles returned.

Alan had thrived in Dakar for a year. The question remained if I could survive for a week.

Upon our arrival a sea of black males, each clamoring to help with our baggage, met us. I was about to take one of them up on his offer when Alan told me sternly, "Hold on to your baggage and follow me to the customs station."

The Cawthons were there to meet us. My survival remained in jeopardy as I wrangled with sleeping au naturel, constantly having to boil water, being the only white surrounded by a sea of black nationals, having the commode and shower lose their power flow at the most inopportune times, and being awakened every morning by the Islamic call to prayer.

The friendly missionaries and national Christians worked overtime to make my week memorable. The beautiful African women, clad in batik-designed clothes, with babes strapped to their backs, intrigued me. The children in Senegal were the same as children everywhere. They bustled with energy, bugged each other, competed for the teacher's attention, and couldn't wait for snack time.

Dakar was to become, for me, more than a place. It became a life-changing experience. My one-week missionary stint ended, and I headed home.

I arrived at Chattanooga on the eve of our new school term. I had to forget the jet lag. There were children to serve, lesson plans to make, and deadlines to meet.

When Alan finished his second term in Senegal, he returned to a family crisis. His dad's angiogram test had led to quadruple by-pass surgery, cardiac arrest, blood clots, and a touch-and-go struggle for life.

Chapter 16

Conditions of the Heart

"For…seven years…I was on call for a possible trip
to the emergency room."

At fifty-five, my secure world was coming unglued. "Help!" I yelled. "Come quickly. My husband is dying."

A team of men dressed in white came lumbering down the hospital corridor bringing with them a big machine. To complicate matters, the cardiac wing that morning was understaffed. One nurse was in a meeting, and the head nurse wasn't even on the floor.

I was angry. I'd gone home for a change of clothes and when I returned, Claude told me he was having pain. I asked, "Have you called the nurses?"

"Yes, but they haven't come."

"Let's call them again," I said.

He picked up the intercom and said, "Nurse, I need something for pain."

The respondent said, "Ok." Still, no one came.

I waited about five minutes and went to the nurses' station. "My husband is in room 705. He's called twice for pain medicine and no one has come." She promised to see about it immediately.

Now it was too late!

A nurse attendant coaxed me into a small room reeking with nicotine and coffee odors. I asked for a phone and called our sons.

I turned around and there stood my pastor. Some may say his coming was sheer happenstance. I beg to differ; God sent him.

By the time the boys arrived we'd received the word, "He's alive! We're taking him to the cardiac care unit."

Claude was to remain in the cardiac critical care unit for ten days. It hurt seeing my husband hooked up to that monstrous machine called a respirator, with its many tubes rammed down his throat.

Friends from Rossville First Baptist made it possible for me to stay in the hospital motel downtown. During his second night in the CCC unit I had a phone call.

"Your husband," said his nurse, has scribbled on a piece of paper the words book and wife. Can you tell me what it means?"

"Yes, he's asking for a Bible. I'll be right down."

I was quite sure he wanted me to read the Shepherd's Psalm. Claude grabbed my hand and held it tightly. Meanwhile, a burden rolled from my shoulders. Not only was my husband alive, but he was mentally alert. Being clinically dead for five minutes usually results in brain damage, so no one in the medical profession was giving us any promises.

They gradually began to wean him off the respirator. He went through a stage of mental confusion, some of which was amusing. Instead of being president of our county educators association, he had me as president of the Georgia Association of Educators.

He kept telling me some deacon was out to get him. I couldn't tell if his foe was from the church he had served for eighteen years or the one where he was now serving on a temporary basis. Anyway, Claude would describe in detail the conniving wiles of his foe.

When some friends from a neighboring town came to visit, he told them to please visit someone else because he needed to sleep. When I kissed him on the cheek I whispered, "Your sugar is so sweet."

"Don't tell the others," he said, motioning toward the nurses, "they'll all be wanting some."

At last it was decision time. Claude was ready to be moved off the ventilator and to breathe on his own. I refused to have him sent to the cardiac floor where he had endured the cardiac arrest. Instead I opted to send him by ambulance to our community hospital in North Georgia.

Claude made the transition fine. However, within a week we were to go through a series of blood clots and attending problems that go with long hospital stays.

Most of his doctors felt his mental ability would be permanently impaired, but I did not. Early on, I recognized the strong impact his medication was having on his ability to think clearly. Some nights he had me preaching, burying the dead, and praying for the sick—right by his bedside.

I'd been on leave from teaching for more than six weeks when we were cleared to come home. Claude had to learn how to walk again. If you've ever seen a grown man groping like a toddler to get from one chair to another, you'll know some of the pressure I was under. He was released from the hospital on Thursday, and it took some tall talking on my part to keep him from preaching the next Sunday morning. In fact, I won by agreeing to let him preach the following Sunday, provided he was steadier on his feet.

Claude had it all worked out. He would sit on a kitchen barstool and preach. God was gracious, and Claude continued daily to improve.

Throwing common sense to the wind, the deacons and I decided to let him have a go at preaching. Needless to say, members of the congregation and I were basket cases until the final "Amen" was said. Claude continued for two months using his barstool perch.

For the following seven years, while teaching special children, I was on call for a possible trip to the emergency room. When the secretary came to my room with the message, "Claude called and needs you to come home," I'd rush my resource children back to their rooms and race home. Claude's needs took priority status.

As for my school children, they all had major problems. Some had loving, supportive parents; others did not know who/where they belonged. A few still believed they could conquer the world; most thought school success was for others, not them. Each required a specialized learning program. That was hard enough to implement, but still harder was getting classroom teachers involved in majoring on each child's strengths while not ignoring their weaknesses.

I often stayed late at school, only to come home laden with work to be checked. Most of all, I labored at developing new strategies to get the job done.

More than one-third of my caseload consisted of children with behavior disorders. I worked with five boys daily for more than half the school day for five years. Behaviorally they would take one step forward and then two backwards. My greatest delight was in seeing many of my children return to their classrooms, able to compete with their peers.

Eventually Claude returned to interim church work, but was still subject, on short notice, to be hospitalized.

Chapter 17

Questions without Answers

"'Amazing Grace' spoke volumes of understanding to my heart."

Completing his two-year assignment in Africa, Alan began graduate studies at the Southern Baptist Theological Seminary in Louisville, Kentucky. As Christmas 1988 approached, I whirled around the house putting finishing touches on my holiday arrangements.

Alan arrived as scheduled and everything seemed destined for a festive week. Little did I suspect that ideas often surfacing in my wildest dreams would soon emerge, making this, my fifty-fifth Christmas, unforgettable. My worst nightmare was about to become reality.

Christmas Day fell on Saturday. Our family—Claude, Max, Alan, and I—gathered for dinner and afterwards exchanged gifts.

On Sunday morning Claude left early for his interim pastor duties at a Baptist church sixty miles away. Alan and I agreed to join him for the worship hour.

As we motored toward our destination, Alan, now twenty-six, seemed wound tighter than a ball of twine. Everything I said or did was wrong. He appeared lost in a world of thought clearly labeled, "Stay Out!"

Alan turned on some classical music. Every time I opened my mouth he reminded me he was listening to the music. His rudeness was out of character. I was baffled. I couldn't put my finger on the trouble. It was obvious something wasn't right.

When I did speak, I told him, "Dad wants you to meet the former pastor's daughter. She'll be playing the piano this morning. Are you interested?"

"No!" he said testily, adding, "I've been down that road too many times and I'm weary of it."

I crawled back into my mother shell, full of questions but saying nothing more.

After lunch Alan and I returned home while his dad stayed to make some hospital visits. Upon our return I retrieved the Sunday newspaper and sat down to read. Alan sat on the couch.

"O.K.," I said, "What's bothering you? I feel like there is a wall between us, and I don't know how it got there. Do you?"

He didn't respond, so I continued, "Tell me why you're seeing a therapist."

"Do you really want to know?"

"Yes, I do."

"Mom, I'm gay."

There was silence. The words I had spent years denying had been spoken. I dropped the paper and rushed to where he sat and threw my arms around him.

His eyes clouded with tears.

"I was afraid you might never touch me again," he said. "Some parents, when they find out their son is gay, refuse to have anything to do with him."

By now we were both crying, each for different reasons. I was crying because I felt Alan had been going down a heart-rending road and hadn't felt free to share his journey with me. Alan, on the other hand, was worried about my ability to cope with his coming out.

"I've wanted for months to tell you, but I never could bring myself to do it. I've even bought books about coming out to parents. I've always known how important I am to you. I've tried with all my heart to live up to your expectations. I've hidden my sexual identity from you because the last thing on the face of this earth I'd ever want to do is hurt you."

"Maybe you aren't really gay," I said. "Isn't there just a tiny possibility you're wrong?"

"No, Mom, I'm gay and nothing is going to change that—it's just part of who I am," he continued. "Correct me if I'm wrong, but your whole life is bound up in your church, your relationship with me, and your work at school."

I nodded my agreement.

Alan continued, "I feel liberated, like for the first time I'm letting the real me out in public. However, I do worry about your ability to handle having a gay son. Your church, Dad, and community all think it is wrong for someone to be gay."

We both decided that, for the time being, we wouldn't tell his dad, who was still recuperating from a massive heart attack. The last thing either of us wanted was to provoke another one.

I continued to probe. "Are you sure? Really sure? I've heard of programs where they claim to deprogram cases of sexual orientation. Money, I assure you, will be no problem."

Alan carefully went over the options, as he saw them.

"I can try to live a celibate life, or I can search for a partner who shares my faith and cultural values. However, there is one thing I absolutely refuse to do and that is to go through deprogramming. It just doesn't work!"

"What if you get AIDS?"

"I'm aware of the risk of HIV and AIDS. Trust me, Mama. The answer lies in having safe sex."

"Tell me about your therapy sessions."

"You'd love my counselor. She reminds me a lot of you. She's warm, accepting, and loving. I've never been happier. It is so important to embrace myself as a gay man."

"I'm so confused," I said. "Right now I don't know what I believe about homosexuality. However, I do know I love and trust you. I always have and I always will."

That night Alan had agreed to play his oboe at a church in our community. He asked me to come along. The service was brief, and Alan's selection of "Amazing Grace" spoke volumes of understanding to my heart. Later when doubt reared its head, I laid claim to "Amazing Grace."

The next day Alan left for Louisville. And what about me? I was left at home, with my tears, restless nights, a crushing heartbreak, and a million "God questions."

My work with and for exceptional children literally became my salvation. Their needs, both critical and demanding, kept my attention focused on them instead of me. In the past I'd been a master at pushing aside the subject of sexual orientation. I had deliberately ignored the telltale signs in Alan's childhood.

Besides, I'd turned Alan's future in this regard over to God and he wouldn't let me down. Or, would he?

I felt like my soul had been tossed in a washing machine on a high-speed cycle that ran way beyond its due time. God had always been my source of refuge, his Word my treasured guide. I wept. I questioned. I pled. I bargained with God. My prayers had been unanswered. Why? Where did I go wrong?

As I looked backward and inward, all the mistakes of my life took on super proportions. There was no denying my son, next to my faith, held center stage in my life.

I walked around in a maze, performing my daily tasks halfheartedly. I didn't do a lot of verbal praying. Instead, my whole being became a plea for divine help. I felt like I was helpless and alone, facing the eye of a hurricane.

I always feel at loose ends when I can't affect change. That's precisely where I found myself. Alan was gay. Period. With no ifs, ands, or buts attached.

Where could I run? How could I blot this conversation from my memory bank? Could I shuck off the Old Testament and cling only to the New Testament?

Casting off my faith was really never an option. Flinging my fists to the heavens and blasting out at God didn't seem appropriate. Could I live in a gray, neutral faith environment? Could I admit there were some questions without answers?

A part of me was too fixated on what others, if they knew, might think. Was my worry for Alan's image or my own? I suspect aspects of both were involved. After all, I prided myself on being a perfect mom. I certainly didn't like the idea of someone downgrading my pride and joy, namely my son, or my role in his development. Why was my son's success so intertwined with my self-image?

My emotions were taking a high-speed roller coaster ride and as hard as I tried, I couldn't find a stopping place. Every time I thought I had things settled, a group of "what ifs" cropped up.

I was plagued with guilt for withholding my conversation from my husband. After all, he had as much at stake in Alan's disclosure as I did. Why didn't I tell him?

This is a question, decades later, I'm still asking. It was partially due to his physical health. At the time of my son's coming out, his dad had recently undergone quadruple by-pass surgery, been clinically dead for five minutes, and had suffered many setbacks before he was finally released.

I lived in a state of anxiety concerning his health. It was not at all uncommon for me to be called home from school for a rush trip to the emergency room. Neither Alan nor I were sure how his sexual orientation would affect his dad.

My silence was partially due to remarks I had heard Claude make from the pulpit and in private. He definitely looked on homosexuality as a sin, albeit one that could be forgiven. All an individual had to do, he felt, was confess his sin and refuse to act on his sexual preference.

My silence had nothing to do with my husband's love for his son. He was a loving, caring father.

Looking back over the years, I think it was basically a matter of trust. I felt like in this instance God had been preparing me throughout my life to deal with such a dilemma. While it wasn't a role I cherished, it was one I could not back away from. Besides, I truly planned, at the right time and place, to level with my husband. That right time never evolved.

Mainly it was because I keenly felt Alan's being gay was tied in with my family tree. My mind flashed back to a time when I was seven.

I felt akin to the Old Testament character Job. I had left no stone unturned in my role as a parent. Perfect? Of course not! However, I did the best I knew to do. From the moment I became pregnant I had prayed for guidance. I wanted to be for my child the mother I always wanted, but never had. No one could ever accuse me of being uninvolved with his growth and development. Perhaps, I thought, I overdid my parenting role.

Alan's sexual preference, like an arrow, remained lodged in my heart. The blame, I felt, was mine, not his. All mine!

"God," I asked, "why are you punishing me? It isn't fair!" I screamed. "God, come on; treat me right."

My Bible and I were constant companions. I became a consummate reader of the Scriptures, especially the New Testament. Meanwhile, Alan held me intact with his phone calls, notes, and books. He constantly absolved me of guilt, assuring me his childhood days were positive and affirming.

Despite his comforting validations, I still asked: "Why, God? Why? Help me make sense of this chaos!"

Feverishly I began rehashing my memories of Alan's childhood. Suppose I had a chance to do it all over again. What would I do differently?

Chapter 18

A Heart at War

"I'm hungry for days of laughter."

There are different kinds of war. On the morning of December 7, 1941, when I was ten, we rode in a wagon less than two miles from the farm to Jordan Methodist Church.

When the service was over, the pastor came home with us for Sunday dinner. Having had their fill of fried chicken, potato salad, green beans, and garden-grown tomatoes, Mama and the preacher retired to the living room.

Flames from our fireplace projected dancing patterns on our bare walls. As the grownups rocked and talked, I jiggled the radio knobs trying to tune in "The Green Hornet." Or was it "Amos 'n' Andy?"

What came from the radio that day turned the world upside down.

"Ladies and gentlemen, we interrupt this program to bring you the President of the United States."

"My fellow Americans," said President Franklin Delano Roosevelt, "December 7, 1941, is a date that will live in infamy. Today, suddenly and without warning, the naval and air force bombers of the Empire of Japan attacked our country. Tomorrow I will ask the Congress of the United States to declare war on Japan."

We sat in stunned silence. Finally the preacher said something like, "I wouldn't have been surprised if we were going to war against Germany. But, Japan? Now we have two enemy countries to fight. Makes you think this old world is about to end."

I was almost eleven and in the fifth grade. Now I had the end of the world to add to my basket of woes. No eleven-year-old wants to entertain thoughts of the world ending.

At other times the wars were within. I was now in my late fifties. Dealing alone with Alan's sexual orientation was difficult. Yet my heart was at war as to whether to share my "Alan secret" with Claude or to wait.

On one occasion it looked as if I had waited too long. I had rushed back from a church meeting to join my husband in watching the World Series in 1987.

"A big earthquake has hit San Francisco," he whispered, his face a picture of despair. Alan and his partner Tom had recently moved from Louisville to San Francisco, and Alan had enrolled at the University of California at Berkeley.

The nature of Alan and Tom's relationship had never been discussed with Claude, but did he know or have clear suspicions? Surely he did.

The waiting game had begun. I stood frozen in space, glaring at the television. Meanwhile, my emotions soared higher than an Alpine mountain. The television set revealed an angry inferno in San Francisco's marina area.

Commentators kept rehashing what might happen if the fire touched off arsenals holding chemicals and gas lines. I stumbled to the couch, my heart pounding faster than a trapped rabbit, to pray and wait.

After a while I found a map of San Francisco. "Alan's apartment is on the other side of town from the marina," I said, breathing a deep sigh.

Then the television began flashing a fifty-foot section of the Oakland Bridge dangling in space. My heart sank and the tension returned.

"Do you suppose Alan was on the bridge when the quake hit?" I asked, knowing Claude didn't have an answer. A dozen possibilities captured my mind, and I could do nothing but pray and wait.

The commentators warned, "Don't tie up our lines of communications by trying to make phone calls. Don't expect your friends and loved ones living in the Bay area to contact you."

"Lord," I prayed, "I can't reach Alan, but you can. He's your child and never out of the orbit of your love. Prepare me for what I may hear in the hours ahead, and please stay here by my side." I waited with each minute seeming like an eternity.

At eleven o'clock the phone rang. It was Tom's sister who lived in South Carolina. "Hello, Mrs. Mason, I'm Tom's sister, and I just talked with Tom via short-wave radio. He and Alan are fine and are at home. Alan will call you as soon as the electricity is restored."

I thanked her and hung up. Claude and I prayed, thanking God for our good news, while asking God to bless the families of those who weren't so fortunate. I made a stab at sleeping, but could not keep myself from returning to the television. The 7.1 earthquake that had hit the Bay area dominated the air waves.

The next morning as I began preparing breakfast, I told Claude, "The odds are a thousand to one, but I'm going to try calling Alan."

The phone lines connected. Shortly, Alan answered the phone. "Hello, Mom," he said, "I'm fine."

That was all I needed to hear. I went on to school, ready to meet the challenges I faced daily as a resource teacher, knowing I may be called home anytime.

I couldn't shake off my secret. Suppose Alan had been an earthquake victim? That would have been a terrible time to share Alan's sexual orientation. I now knew there would never be an opportune time. Perhaps when Alan came home again the two of us would tell Claude.

Phone calls and letters from Alan, prayer and Bible verses kept my juggling going. How could I justify my son's sexual orientation when the major bodies of Christendom condemned it and supported their views with Scripture?

I decided to take another look at the passages involved and let the chips fall where they may.

Claude chose his seventieth birthday as the time for his retirement from the Rossville pastorate in 1979. He had understood from several deacons, in an unwritten agreement, that when we retired we would be given the manse as a thank-you for eighteen years of faithful service.

They must have had a memory lapse, and Claude had no legal means of holding them to their promise. Fortunately we had bought a lot earlier and had paid for it. To say the least, our savings were meager.

To amplify our problems, the pulpit committee came up with a recommendation for a new pastor while I rushed to Savannah because Mama was very sick.

By the time I got back, the new pastor and his family were ready to move in the parsonage. Meanwhile, all of our belongings were dumped into a business/rental house complex. We lived, perhaps existed is a better description, out of boxes for several months while the builders worked around the clock to erect our house. Soon the house began taking shape. Claude worked daily, and I put in my share of labor when it came to painting.

As the months evolved into years, Claude continued to be a popular interim pastor. Our son, Max, a pharmacist, was married and the father of our grandchild, Patrick. As for me, I renewed an earlier interest in creative writing and retired in 1993 after thirty years of teaching.

In addition to giving me more time to write, my retirement enabled me to give quality time to my husband, whose death was eminent. Finally the time came when he made his next-to-last visit to the emergency room, and wound up staying a week. He came home for two months, but never got over his congestion and pneumonia.

It was during his last stay at home that I penned the following words:

> I yearn for someone or something to pierce through the gray fog of
> my dismay, for someone to make me smile. I'm hungry today for
> days of laughter, for someone to take command, to free me, to bathe
> me in a riot of sunlight. Oh, to be a child again, oblivious to the
> woes of aging.

The dreamer and realist within me are at war. My inner me wants peace, but my outer me courts disaster. My mind recites the ancient creed of the faithful, but my heart wallows in self-pity and expects the worst. Yet, a tremor of hope still beats. I can't and I won't let go of life without a fight.

Death's bony finger crowds me. I feel him breathing down my neck. I tremble at his nearness. I shove him aside and run for the sunshine of wellness. A gamut of alternatives plays like a nonstop video through the corridors of my brain. However, I can't push the reset button or mute the sobs. The tears gush like raging rapids. I'm not ready for the dream to end.

Life is fragile. Yesterday, Claude was robust with the strength of Hercules. I watched the strands of a tightrope begin to fray. I know not when I viewed the first straggled edges. But I've noted each unwinding strand and am learning how age intimidates resilience. The mind and the heart want to fight, but the body says, "Enough, I can go no further."

I watch a body totter instead of walk, as unsure of its next step as a toddler on his maiden journey; a body once exploding with energy; one whose embrace could calm my wildest fears.

Despite our best efforts, death came calling. As he had throughout our marriage, Claude did everything he could to make his exit easier on me. As his condition worsened, he insisted we go over his funeral plans and that I write out his obituary.

Frederick Buechner in his book, *Whistling in the Dark*, sums up my Claude thoughts:

When you remember me, it means that you have carried something of who I am with you, that I have left some mark of who I am on who you are. It means that you can summon me back to your mind even though countless years and miles may stand between us. It means that if we meet again, you will know me. It means that even after I die, you can still see my face and hear my voice and speak to me in your heart.

Seldom a day passes without me remembering a touch, a laugh, a hug that Claude and I shared. It is then I feel he's right in the room with me.

While going through the stages of grief I continued doing the things I had been doing—including my coordination of the children's activities at Rossville First Baptist Church and freelance writing.

However, there were bumps in the road. For starters I succeeded in locking myself out of my house, leaving my house keys in the backdoor entrance, acquiring a big-time case of poison ivy, spending endless days looking for my husband's truck title, fiendishly manicuring our backyard, and proving I was no match for my husband's riding mower.

Yet immediately after Claude's death I had another "Fear not I am with you" moment. For as long as I can remember I'd been afraid of being alone at nighttime. But here I was alone and not afraid. This particular fear had been totally erased. This grace gift began the first night of Claude's homegoing and has continued with me ever since.

After returning to California a week after the funeral, Alan called regularly. So did Max, who lived in the Chattanooga area. Both of my sons were very supportive.

Having a group of children at church who needed quality time and energy was good for me. But don't tell me that God doesn't have a sense of humor.

Since we had only a handful of children belonging to our church family at that time, several of us had begun a bus ministry to bring in other children. One family in particular was more than a handful.

I laughed aloud when, the first Sunday after my retirement from teaching school, a boy named Adam and his two brothers appeared as I drove into the church driveway. One of my most pleasurable aspects of retirement was not dealing with Adam. However, God had other plans. Adam's family had moved within a stone's throw of our church. I was given another opportunity to reach out to a child who had worn my good nature into a tailspin.

My beloved cocker spaniel, Blacky, and I became inseparable. We roamed over a major portion of nearby Chickamauga National Military Park, the first and largest of its kind.

My writing efforts were growing and demanding. In addition to self-editing, I took two courses from the Institute of Children's Literature.

The sense that Claude was gone but not really gone is difficult to explain to those who deal only in the visible present tense. Let's face it. There's nothing more final than a dead corpse. However, Claude and I both subscribed to the belief that the grave was not the end but one's entry into another world ruled solely by our heavenly father in a kingdom where we'd be more alive than ever before.

Rest assured, I haven't had heavenly visitors or visions. However, I often do have a sense that Claude is very near to encourage my noble efforts and yes, sometimes to chide my choices.

I never felt his presence more strongly than when I decided to sell our house and move to Alexian Village atop Signal Mountain north of Chattanooga. It took a while to settle in a new community and find a new circle of friends.

The following year, 2008, God burst through with a delightful surprise. One day during the Advent season at First Baptist Church of Chattanooga, I picked up a devotional guide and read it.

Then I found the editor's name and email address and submitted some monologues I had written. One thing led to another until I became the proud author of two paperback books: *Advent Monologues* and *Lenten Monologues*.

Chapter 19

My Turn at Bravery

"What I had dreaded would bring condemnation brought blessings."

At some point during his first year in Louisville in 1987, Alan had asked for extra money to see a therapist. He didn't divulge his reason and I didn't ask. I was afraid to find out. I had a gut feeling it had to do with sexuality.

I was equally certain that, with counseling, whatever was bothering him would be resolved. Never mind the fact he was twenty-five and had never had a serious romantic encounter. I believed my son would emerge from his counseling straight and not gay and that God would see to it.

After one year at the seminary, Alan transferred to the University of Louisville and began a master's program in oboe performance. His friend Jan was also living in Louisville, and they did lots of things together. It was natural for me to suppose they had serious intentions toward one another back then.

After Alan told me he was gay, however, I wrestled with the issue from a different perspective: honesty. But it was not easy. It took twenty years longer for me to come out as the mother of a gay son.

Why had I been so hesitant? Partially it was because I lived in a small town and had to contend with small-town attitudes about sex and morality. Partially it was because nothing on the national front made it easier. Gays and lesbians in the military were told it was okay to be different sexually, provided they kept it to themselves.

Mostly, however, it was my church life that held me in its shackles of fear. My Southern Baptist view of Scripture made me tremble when I read those dreadful, unconditional statements in Leviticus, and I didn't find much comfort in some of the writings of Saint Paul.

I've heard many people list the great sins. Right at the top along with abortion and the evils of Saddam Hussein ranked being gay or lesbian. These voices were generous in forgiving gay and lesbian persons who will confess their sexual orientation as being sinful and thus denounce their lifestyle. However, hell fire and damnation are pronounced upon those who consider their behavior to be God-given and therefore both healthy and normal.

Southern Baptists have become quite notorious for their condemnation of gays and lesbians. Some have even implied that AIDS is God's punishment for "sinful" behavior. Often they cover their real politics by saying pious things such as "Love the sinner, but hate the sin."

As a pastor's wife, I was affirmed when I helped children from broken hetero-sexual marriages. My Christian friends were responsive to a degree. They gave me money and left me to do the work.

The cooperation stopped when I suggested to a group of churchwomen that we get involved in helping people with AIDS. I could have sworn someone had thrown me into a deep freezer! Not one person of our group of fifteen said a word in response to my suggestion. Their silence spoke volumes.

It seems to me that often in religious circles we tiptoe around unpleasant subjects, rarely having the courage to face them head on. After all, it's more fun to discuss our latest diets or the escapades of our grandchildren.

Meanwhile, I remained in the closet as the parent of a gay son. When I visited my son on the West Coast I felt free, accepting, and open. I was proud to be his mom and to meet his gay friends. Back home in Georgia, I rebottled my emotions and went back in the closet.

As time passed, I grew weary of being in the closet as the parent of a gay son. That's when I told my stepson and my two sisters about my son's gayness. Their warm responses led me to be more courageous.

Shortly thereafter, and in a new and more progressive church setting, I shared my news with my Bible discussion leader. Gradually I bared my soul to about fifteen others in my church. With each revelation I was met with acceptance and love. No one suggested my son be deprogrammed or that he had the sign of the beast embedded in his forehead. Furthermore, none of them condemned my role as a parent.

I attended my fiftieth college reunion back in Texas in April 2003. Two of my college friends met me in Waco, where I was staying with one of my son's university professors, and drove me to Belton.

For forty-eight hours we hugged, laughed, ate, took pictures, and talked inces-santly. Finally it was time to return to Waco. I don't know what possessed me, but just before we got to Waco I blurted out, "I want the two of you to know my son is gay."

My friend's responses were quick and to the point: "I have no problem with that," followed by a quick, "Neither do I."

That, for me, was a miracle. When I returned home to Georgia, I wondered if I had the courage to break the news to other college friends whom I had known and cherished for fifty-three years. That's when my eye caught the message on a pillow my son and his partner had given me earlier that year. It read:

Let me get this straight. My grandchild is a dog?

I chose ten friends of my college years and wrote them the following note:

My Pillow's Secret

An inscription on one of my bed pillows reads, "Let me get this straight. My grandchild is a dog?" For more than fifteen years I've known my beloved son is gay. I've wanted to share this with you, my friends, for a long, long time. I held back because I worried over what your reactions might be. However, the older I get, the more I realize I cannot control what others think or do. Please know that spiritually Alan and I have long ago received acceptance, peace, grace, and love from our Lord. Alan is one of my best friends, my keenest writing critic, my enabler, and helper.

My Prayer

Thank you, Father, for my friends
Who laugh when I laugh,
Who cry when I cry,
Who rejoice with me in good times,
Who hold my hand during the storms.
Thank you, Father, for my friends.

Through many dangers, toils, and snares,
we have already come.
Tis grace that has brought us safe thus far,
and grace will lead us on.

With that assurance I close.

—Amen and Amen

I wasn't prepared spiritually or emotionally for the overwhelming positive responses that came flooding my way. I was like a kid on a blistering summer day getting a triple-dipped ice cream cone. Telephone calls and letters came from career missionaries, staunch Southern Baptists, and a sprinkling of those with more liberal leanings.

Most of them shared some of their own family challenges and fears. Snippets of their comments include:

> *I've long known you have God's peace and love because your life reveals it.*

> *We all have had so many hurts and disappointments.*

> *I'm so glad you have a good relationship with your son.*

> *That's the nice part of being over seventy. At this point in our lives we know that God is so wonderful and that loving our children unconditionally is the only way to happiness.*

> *You have a Godlike spirit.*

> *I love you very much and admire you more with each new mountain you climb and every valley you walk through. I see Christ in your life. May God bless you and Alan.*

> *Thank you for sharing "My Pillow Secret." I'm sure it was not easy for you to share such news with others. My grandchild is a boat. With classmates talking about grandchildren and the joy they bring, it is not easy to accept the fact that grandchildren are not in your future—nor in mine. There is a lot we do not know about homosexuality, but the homosexuals I know are sensitive, artistic, loving individuals.*

The question uppermost in my mind was why I had waited so long. What I had dreaded would bring condemnation brought blessings. What I thought might result in sermonettes abounded in affirmations. I cried tears of joy as I thanked God again and again.

It remained to be seen what my next step would be. The first recipients of my disclosure were mostly Texans, living a thousand miles away from my native Georgia. What would it be like to share my pillow's secret to those locally who knew me as a pastor's wife, church worker, and friend? I owed it to myself and to them to be candid.

My next target group became friends from the church where my husband had served for eighteen years, and where I had been immersed for thirty years prior to joining another congregation. I revised my Texas letter and sent it to ten of them.

This time it was to people who had been friends of my family since Alan was one year old. Many of them were people who I had heard shower dispersions on what they deemed deviant sexual behavior. Would I hear from any of them? If I did, what kind of responses would I see?

The day after I mailed my letters I had a phone call from one of the recipients assuring me that both Alan and I would always be a part of the special memories she held dear, adding, "It's a loving heart that brings a glow of beauty to all things."

I received affirming phone calls and numerous notes. Three of my friends made no overt response but continued to interact with me as if they never got my note. For them, I suspect, the issue of homosexuality is still a taboo subject.

Two of the responses were from deacons.

Dear Lynelle,

We were touched that you would share your feelings with us. Thank you for your confidence in us.

I think of Alan and I smile. The five-year-old in preschool Sunday school who sang so beautifully, "God is so good, God is so good, God is so good. He's so good to me."

God made us all, and we are all different, and God has a purpose for us all. I think of Alan's spiritual gifts, especially his music, his personality, his giving spirit. God is so good.

When Claude was our pastor and you supported him as no other pastor's wife in our church has, we grew to love the three of you—Claude, Lynelle, and Alan—nothing has changed. You are a part of our lives that we cherish. Our children grew up during that time in that church. Claude married Bob and Lynda, Eyleen and Alex; he baptized our Jan and buried her. Jan and Alan were good friends.

You can't throw those memories away. There are some narrow-minded people who will hurt you. Pray for them. I do.

You are a joy. Good luck with your writing.

Dear Lynelle,

Thank you for having enough confidence in us to share your secret. Let me comfort you by telling you up front: nothing you shared with us changes how we feel about you and Alan. We love, appreciate, and respect both of you just as much now as we did before you shared your "Pillow Secret."

I'm so glad you decided to share this with your friends. Now you will know we are your friends "no matter what and through thick and thin."
We love you!

That led me to yet another group. I was getting good at coming out! How about my current church fellowship? I decided to begin with my Bible study group of fifty-plus members. Ten or more of my class members had previously read portions of a memoir I've written, "Living with Questions—an Evolving Faith." However, most of my class didn't know about my son's gayness.

I left the time and type of disclosure to our leader. She decided to have six copies of "My Pillow's Secret" available for members to read.

Several months passed and "My Pillow's Secret" was still circulating. Once again I have received many positive, encouraging remarks. One of the deacons, who is also a member of our class, said, "I've always thought highly of you, but now my opinion of you is even greater."

It would be naïve for me to believe everyone agrees with me on issues of gender and homosexuality. However, following traditional southern mores, those who have a problem with my tenets are, at the present, noncommittal.

I learned a valuable lesson from this experience: Should you find yourself harboring something you think you can't share with others, put your best friends to the test. Perhaps, like me, you'll be surprised by their acceptance and understanding. Burden sharing comes straight from the New Testament.

I've come out of the closet. How about you?

Chapter 20

A Faith House Crumbles

"Since moving to Alexian Village, I've committed three cardinal
Baptist sins: I've taken dancing lessons, drunk my share of wine,
and played Bingo for cash."

In some odd way, the Southern Baptist Convention had become family to me—perhaps a surrogate parent in my mind. Not only has my life been heavily invested in Southern Baptist churches, but also I attended Southern Baptist camps and educational institutions, served in Southern Baptist mission programs, and have written for Southern Baptist publications.

So my larger story cannot be understood apart from the pain and shock I experienced when leadership of the Southern Baptist Convention was taken over by Christian fundamentalists beginning in the late seventies. This dismantling of my denominational home coincided with the disclosure of my son's sexual orientation and my husband's heart problems, accentuating all of them.

With a little time and distance, however, I realize that the Southern Baptist Convention probably never was what I envisioned it to be. How else can I explain what has happened to it over the last thirty years?

Fundamentalism seems like an easy word to define. It has to do with adhering to the basics. When it comes to religion, it means subscribing to basic tenets that are essential to the Christian experience. However, don't question a single basic belief—or you are in trouble.

How can two art connoisseurs study a great painting and appreciate its beauty from totally different perspectives? How can two travelers go entirely different routes, with both arriving at the same destination? In the same vein, how can two Christians read a selected passage of Scripture and arrive at two different conclusions?

Fundamentalists say there is one, and only one, correct response to a given passage: theirs. Other Christians, including me, have been known to differ with them.

The word "fundamentalist" was not in my preteen vocabulary. Yet, I suspect, my early religious indoctrination was from those with fundamentalist leanings.

Church life in rural South Georgia was uncomplicated. All I was ever exposed to were the Baptists and the Methodists. Each congregation met once a month.

Preaching services and altar calls were long. Time wasn't urgent in those days. Few people had a watch, and most folks, after church was over, were going home.

The preacher's job, I think, was to make us feel guilty of our sins through vivid demonstrations of people in hell. These preachers ranted and raved as they got across to us how bad we really were.

The altar call consisted of a time when people made responses to the sermon. Often the same people came forward, sometimes confessing the same sins every Sunday.

The preacher had little or no religious training, but that was in his favor. Bible training schools for pastors were frowned upon. Education, in general, wasn't a thing to be treasured.

Another aspect of churchgoing was the music or, more aptly, the lack of it. My Aunt Bell, Mama's sister, never got in a hurry. Aunt Bell was the church organist for the Methodists. She'd pump and squeeze on that old organ, and then we'd commence to sing—kind of. The tempo of our singing always matched Aunt Bell's slow pacing.

The Baptists, without an organist or pianist, were worse off. Some guy would get up and signal the Stamps Baxter notes to get us started and we'd all join in.

Revival meetings today, even among Baptists, are short-lived or non-existent. In my preteen days they often lasted for three weeks and were usually in the late summer, after crops had been laid back. Meeting every night for three weeks was long enough for the worst of sinners to get revived.

Churchgoing was largely a community building and sharing time. It was a place where friends and family gathered, shared stories, and helped one another in times of need.

Modern fundamentalists give credence to the Bible as the inerrant, infallible Word of God. In the late 1970s the word "inerrant" sent lots of folk scurrying to the dictionary. The word infallible had been around for Baptists for a long time. Infallible for most Southern Baptists was what the Catholics called their pope.

Some would say the fundamentalist stance on the Bible amounts to "bibliolatry," or worship of the Bible.

For a long time I've had trouble understanding Paul's view on women. He seems to contradict himself, or else his theology grew as he responded to human needs.

In 1 Timothy 2:11 he tells women to be silent in the church and if they have anything to say, to tell it to their husband and let him, in turn, tell it to the church.

Saint Paul goes back to his thoughts on Adam and Eve. The woman was deceived, not Adam. Redemption comes to her through childbearing.

Yet in Galatians 3:26-28 he speaks of the equality of all people, regardless of gender or nationality. In other passages, he praises women who served along with him in his missionary endeavors. He even gives Phoebe the possible status of pastor or deaconess in Romans 16:1. At any rate Paul, as a key leader of the church at Cenchra, endorses Phoebe.

Many Southern Baptists in local congregations could care less whether moderate or fundamentalist leaders control the seminaries or mission work. They are, at best, pseudo-fundamentalists. Unlike me, they weren't locked into denominational programs and position statements.

Their main loyalty is to the local church, oftentimes the self-same church of their parents and grandparents. They simply are not consistent enough in their beliefs and practices to be dyed-in-the-wool fundamentalists. They tend to fudge on interpretation when it gets too close to home.

I don't have trouble with the things fundamentalists believe. Every Christian has the right to interpret the Bible as she or he sees fit. I do have a problem with the manner in which fundamentalists often implement their beliefs.

Many are autocratic and bombastic in stating their beliefs. To be a Christian, from their viewpoint, is to believe as they believe. There can be no exceptions.

If someone questions the virgin birth of Jesus, he or she is not a Christian. If someone questions that the creation of the heavens, including planet earth, may have taken longer than seven days, then he or she is a heretic, not a true believer.

Yet, most women in fundamentalist churches do not toe the line completely when it comes to the rigid enforcement of biblical statements. They spend hours at beauty shops, health salons, and fashion stores, not to mention the money they spend on jewelry. I suggest they re-study 1 Timothy 2:9.

Biblical literalism is difficult to follow. Paul and the members of the early church felt that the return of Jesus was imminent. Paul even laid claim as to how Jesus' return to earth will be played out (see 1 Thess. 4:13-18).

Yet, in 1 Thessalonians 5:1, Paul relies on the words of Jesus when he says that our Lord's return will resemble the coming of a thief in the night. One would be hard pressed to believe that 2,000 years fall within the imminent time frame.

The book of Revelation, when taken as story, is a powerful reminder that in the end, those who follow God's way will be victors. When taken literally, you get all kinds of millennium (end-of-the-world) views and time charts.

Most fundamentalist Christians hold strong beliefs on certain social issues. They feel they have a mandate from God for the stands they take. Their litmus test includes being against a woman's right to choose abortion, opposing gay rights, supporting Christian prayer in public schools, and breaking down the wall that separates church and state.

Since the rise of the Moral Majority in the 1970s, many Christian fundamentalist groups have joined forces with the Republican Party. This works well in most southern states, but sometimes creates a problem for Republicans in other regions.

Historically, Baptists have been reluctant to join with other groups on any issue—with the notable exception having been the temperance movement. Today they are politically aligned with any group that promotes their litmus test and political agenda.

The remaking of my denominational home into a fundamentalist convention was like hearing a loved one had a terminal sickness. You didn't know how long it would be before the demise, but sooner or later, you knew death would come calling.

I began reading everything I could buy on the Southern Baptist controversy, from all perspectives. As I read the thoughts of others, I asked myself, "What do I believe?"

In 1984 I wrote this summation of my beliefs:

> *I agree with the fundamentalists on the virgin birth of Jesus, although he could have been born otherwise and I would still call him Lord.*
>
> *I totally agree with fundamentalists on the resurrection of Jesus and that, through his death, he paid my "sin debt" in full.*
>
> *I agree with fundamentalists that Jesus will come back to earth again. I probably have strong differences with them on the how, when, and why of his reappearance.*
>
> *The area where I completely part company with the fundamentalists is their tenet that the Bible is inerrant and infallible, denying all scientific theories, historical, geographical, and cultural pronouncements that run counter to the biblical message. They accept only a literal, verbal view of the Bible.*
>
> *There is no book comparable to my Bible. From Genesis to Revelation it reveals to me a loving God on mission to redeem his greatest creation, mankind. However, I do not go to my Bible to learn the fine points of science, history, economics, or current events.*
>
> *How then, do I use my Bible?*
>
> *I go to my Bible to learn who created the earth and mankind. Science deals with the how of creation. I see no conflict between the two bodies of learning. Who and how are two separate questions.*
>
> *I go to my Bible to discover how God related in ancient times to individuals and nations. I refuse to "play God." Since the original authors, whoever they might have been, are no longer among us, it seems to me unwise for some among us to declare they know*

exactly how and why these original manuscripts came into being.
When God chose to reveal his divine message, he was not forced to
strip the writers of their individuality or to erase the influence of
the time frame in which they lived.

I go to my Bible to find the individual relationship I can have
with God. I go to my Bible to see all mankind through God's lens.
I believe God reveals himself progressively in Scripture. Jesus affords
us God's greatest and sharpest revelation of himself.

As a teenager, I was taught to filter any questionable passages
in the Old Testament through the teachings of Jesus. My clearest
picture of who God is, what God is like, and what God expects of
me is seen in the life, death, and resurrection of Jesus, my Lord.

I go to my Bible to find out how my Lord wants me to live.
Jesus lived among us as one who served. If I am to be like him, then
I, too, must be a servant to all.

I go to my Bible for enlightenment and encouragement in the
face of tremendous personal, national, and international problems.
I don't always find neatly packaged answers in Scripture, but I do
find guiding principles and abounding support.

My metamorphosis from a blind follower of the Southern Baptist Convention to a place where I started thinking for myself didn't happen overnight. It started when Bible professors in college and seminary required more of their students than the regurgitation of facts. They focused a great deal of attention to times in which a given Bible book was written.

Racism was a big issue in the late fifties. My professors inspired us to apply biblical principles to present-day social problems. That is a far cry, incidentally, from providing one with foolproof texts to support a given ideology.

By the time I graduated from the seminary in 1956, I had become a strong advocate of women's rights and civil rights for African Americans. Without my knowing it, God was working behind the scenes in my behalf, laying the foundation that would enable me later on to accept my son's sexual orientation.

My integrity, thanks be to God, is not determined by a fundamentalist mindset. Who I am in Christ is as viable today as it was thirty years ago. Nor has my desire to help those who have little or no voice in the world's marketplace waned.

The Scriptures admonish, "Be joyful always; pray continually; give thanks in all circumstances, for this is God's will for you in Christ Jesus" (1 Thess. 5:18).

I never thought I'd be grateful, despite the heartbreak or the vast changes in the Southern Baptist Convention. But while I still regret it happened and feel deeply that it was a wrong move, the things that have evolved in my life thereafter have been a blessing to my spiritual journey.

The loss of one spiritual home has given me the chance to become part of new ones. It makes me feel like being a child up for adoption and getting to pick my parents.

For one, the First Baptist of Chattanooga, Tennessee, offers me an opportunity to choose from among twenty hands-on projects where I can witness to the living Christ in our community. Many within my church family accept me as a fellow pilgrim. Some embrace my support of my gay son while others, who may differ, refuse to be judgmental.

My encouragers come from my Sunday Bible class, my fellow Stephen ministers, the library staff, the teachers of conversational English, the international students, my seven-member "Companions in Christ" prayer support group, and others.

The first church members to recruit me to be a part of their group were the workers with conversational English for internationals. I attended their meetings and became actively involved with a Kurdish family. My bonding with the Kurdish mother and her young children was instant. This family allowed me to combine my teaching skills, my missionary zeal, and my love to help a family unfamiliar with American culture.

Later I took training to become a teacher of conversational English to internationals. Through this work I established a positive relationship with persons from Iran and Poland. When I teach conversational English, I am never sure which of us learns the most. I suspect it is I.

Again and again I have discovered the joy that seems to always follow pain.

Chapter 21

More Strong Women

"Friendships flourish when treated with kind words and hugs."

The mark of strong women on my life can be seen from my earliest days to the present. It is impossible to point to every woman and every area of influence, but I will share a few more.

Idella Bodie birthed my writing career. I met her when I was attending my second writer's conference at Epworth by the Sea on Saint Simons Island in Georgia. Somehow she learned about a children's manuscript I had written, and that had been sent to a reviewer of adult stories.

Idella stopped everything she was doing and gave me a line-by-line critique of my manuscript at no cost to me. I instinctively sensed she was someone who genuinely cared for those of us wannabe writers.

From then on, I couldn't get enough of Idella. I had so much to learn and for some reason, she saw something of worth in me. She gave me courage to continue writing. I took every course she taught and bugged her endlessly via emails.

If I close my eyes, I can see her sparkling brown eyes and smile. I can feel her standing next to me going over certain obvious points again and again. She never turned me down, and I'm most grateful.

I've re-read her young adult book *Carolina Girl* several times. Here comes that God-hunger bit again. Our life stories are made of many common threads leading me to conclude that if she could make it, then so could I.

I am constantly editing my work and deeply believe I have stories to share. I keep Idella's comments on what constitutes a story/manuscript attached to my computer desk.

Idella didn't simply tell me I was missing the mark in my writing. She explained the missing elements and offered suggestions. She always left me thinking I was getting better and better and encouraged me to keep working.

Martha Killian was sent to me while I struggled secretly with the issue of Alan's sexual orientation and openly with Claude's multiple heart problems. At least three teachers preceded the coming of Martha to the position she assumed.

Martha had entered the teaching profession for the specific purpose of making a positive difference with children. She stood less than five feet tall even when wearing heels. Martha had big, expressive eyes, a soft voice, a ready smile, and an infectious chuckle. Within a month I knew I'd met my match.

Martha loved each of the children and forcibly became their advocate. Often she was at loggerheads with derelict parents, classroom teachers, central staff personnel, and government agencies. Since the above also described my status, I relished her input.

On one occasion she relentlessly informed the local police department of a certain house where one of her pupils lived that needed to be condemned. One afternoon she drove me to the house in question. For me it became a horror trip —and it wasn't even Halloween. We had to step gingerly over dog deposits, dirty dishes on the floor, and a dreadful odor that had been months in the making.

Martha told the mother what the police department was going to do, and the mother flew into a rage, yelling, "How we live is none of your damn business!"

I was relieved when we left. The house was condemned. Later the parents divorced. Meanwhile, the mother discovered soap, got a steady job as a grocery clerk, and became the breadwinner for her family.

Long after Martha had moved with her family to another state, I had the privilege of monitoring this case more closely. Imagine my surprise one day when at the checkout counter I was met by the child Martha had originally gone to bat for. There she was ready to ring up my groceries. I'm convinced this would never have happened if Martha hadn't insisted on changes.

When I needed moral support Martha became my anchor. Whatever the problem, Martha was both my sounding board and cheerleader. She was a fresh wind of hope in a profession high with burnout. The two of us moved as one on major issues.

We planned together, sometimes we cried, and when things got all screwed up we'd laugh. This was no polite giggle. We laughed uncontrollably. The laughter released our frustrations and served as a constant reminder of our own fallibility.

Martha and I were teaching together while my son Alan served as a missionary journeyman in Senegal, West Africa, as well as during my husband's initial heart problems and when my son told me he was gay. In those days I never talked with Martha about Alan being gay; I didn't have to.

Years later when I did tell her she said, "I know and I love both of you." Subject closed.

Martha taught me that scars inflicted while defending the rights of children are negotiable in heaven and that while laughter can't cure everything, it sure makes the distasteful more palatable. Martha is one of my rarest treasures.

Hanging on the wall in my Alexian Village apartment is a poem she gave me. It reads:

> *I believe that imagination is stronger than knowledge.*
> *That myth is more potent than history.*
> *That dreams are more powerful than facts.*
> *That hope always triumphs over experience.*
> *That laughter is the only cure for grief.*
> *And, I believe that love is stronger than death.*
>
> —*Author unknown*

Helen Holmes Ruchti and I were an unlikely twosome. She was everything I wanted to be but wasn't. I was a college freshman; she was a senior. The name Helen Holmes stood for integrity, scholarship, and religious authenticity.

She was easily the number-one student on the campus of Mary Hardin-Baylor. That she bothered to spend time with the likes of me was one of God's gifts of affirmation.

I've often wondered what would have happened to me if she had turned out to be a charlatan. In my mind she was kind of like the pope. Helen could do no wrong. In my freshman college yearbook she wrote:

> *Lynelle, keep on with your head in the clouds—it's closer to heaven.*
> *But keep your feet on the ground so you can walk the steps He trod.*

Sixty years later, I still think that's good advice.

We continued to correspond after college. She went to the now defunct Carver School for Women in Louisville, Kentucky, and married William C. Ruchti.

Helen next appeared on my radar after she won a contest paying her way to Rome, Italy. Since they were living in Rome, Georgia, at the time, she titled her winning entry, "From Rome to Roma."

Then later, the Foreign Mission Board of the Southern Baptist Convention appointed Helen and W. C. as missionaries to the English-speaking congregation in Rome, Italy.

Years passed and once again our paths crossed. Helen spoke during a world missions conference at Burning Bush Baptist Church in Ringgold, Georgia, where my husband was serving as interim pastor. I learned during her visit that she and W. C. had retired to Rome, Georgia, less than fifty miles from my home in Rossville.

Through the deaths of our spouses we were there for each other mainly through correspondence. I sent a copy of "My Pillow's Secret" to Helen and received back an affirming note. Coming as it did from my college hero and a career foreign missionary, it was a deep blessing.

We decided in 2002 to exchange manuscripts and chose Dalton, Georgia, as our contact point. Helen was working on a manuscript combining Italian recipes and devotional thoughts, and I was working on the first draft of my memoir.

We critiqued each other's work. She went on to submit her work to a publisher—only to have the publisher she was working with go out of business. I'm hoping for a better outcome.

Helen Holmes Ruchti taught me to strive for excellence in mind, body, and spirit and never to be content with second best. She taught me that following in the steps of Jesus means to care for those society calls misfits.

Mary Jayne Allen is the former education minister at the First Baptist Church of Chattanooga, Tennessee. I met her before joining that congregation in 1998, when I was involved with a Round Table Book Club of which she was a member.

Whether she's preaching or teaching, sharing with a few or speaking before a large crowd, the characteristics that define her are the same. Mary Jayne is intelligent, disciplined, committed, reflective, loving, gracious, and inclusive. If you share a confidence with her, you can rest assured she'll not tell it to others.

One of the rich experiences of my adult life came when Mary Jayne, along with Carolyn Dobson and Ray Fox, became my Stephen Minister advisors. Participating in this long, intense program with its goal to walk alongside someone experiencing a great grief continues to enrich my spiritual journey daily.

Mary Jayne began introducing to our church family the concept of spiritual formation with a study called "Companions in Christ." Through participation in these studies I am continually learning to be spiritually honest and growing a healthy appetite for listening and quietness in my prayer life.

There have been times when we've been drawn together by mutual wounds inflicted by the actions or words of others. These experiences have bonded our friendship to an even deeper level.

Mary Jayne has taught me that surface thinking and knee-jerk responses aren't on the radar of spiritual formation. I'm learning that spiritual formation is an ongoing process and that self-forgiveness precedes being able to forgive others.

June Holland McEwen is someone I had heard of before we ever met. She had often been quoted in the church news section of *The Chattanooga Times* in the 1980s, in regard to the upheaval within the Southern Baptist Convention. Since we shared mutual views, I appreciated her willingness to pen her opinions and not to be taken aback by those who didn't agree.

Our appreciation of each other picked up a notch when I joined the Round Table Book Club at Chattanooga's First Baptist Church that she and Rolena Ingram co-sponsored.

People like June, with no fault of their own, make people like me feel inferior.

June can read a book while I'm still scanning the book jacket. The questions she asks in giving a book review often make me feel like I haven't read the same book. I'm still looking to find an area of learning where she is not knowledgeable.

If she doesn't know the answer to a question, she's comfortable in saying, "I don't know but I'll look it up." June is a no-frills kind of person. She enjoys sharing a gusty laugh, good food, and finding out the latest church news.

In addition to being a ferocious and eclectic reader, she enjoys sewing, doing all sorts of word puzzles, and keeping in close contact with her children.

June became my Sunday school teacher when I joined First Baptist of Chattanooga. She enjoyed getting us to discuss our views, and rarely was there a time I didn't have something to say. Those were happy, learning, sharing days.

Early on, I chose to tell June my son was gay. I don't remember her exact words. What I do remember is that when some members of our Sunday school started in on gay jokes one Sunday, she simply said something to the effect: "Leave off the gay jokes. A member of our class has a gay son." The jokes stopped, and I've never heard another one.

When I got to the place where I wanted to share about my son with members of my Sunday school class, once again I confided in June. We came up with the section of my memoir where Alan comes out to me and I share my reactions. We made six copies and put them on a table for members to check out and read at their leisure.

I would be amiss to say June and I have always seen everything eye to eye. In times of disagreement, however, we've refused to let it damage our appreciation of each other. Both of us subscribe to the soul competency of the believer doctrine that gives us the privilege and responsibility for our beliefs and actions.

Today we live in the same retirement community and eat Sunday dinner together. Strong friendships outlast a storm of differences.

Rolena Ingram and I met in a water aerobics class at the downtown Chattanooga YMCA. When she found out I was the wife of a minister, she quipped, "You're too happy to be a preacher's wife. Most of the ones I know are on the serious side."

It's hard for me to think of Rolena without thinking of her soul mate—Frank. Whether in the pool or at church, you never saw Rolena without seeing Frank and vice versa. However, in keeping with the theme of this chapter, I'm going to major on Rolena.

After we paddled around in the YMCA pool that day, we talked. Soon we were swapping stories, especially Baptist stories. Before long, we knew enough about each other to fill a small book.

Rolena invited me to the book club, and I readily accepted. Over the years we have shared our writing efforts. Soon she was critiquing everything I wrote.

At one of our round table meetings, after I'd been attending for more than a year, she announced to the group, "I've about given up on Nell. I don't think she's ever going to join our church."

I laughed along with the rest of the group, but when I got home I did some serious thinking and praying. I'd known for several years I needed to align myself with others who cherished their Baptist roots and worked to cultivate them. At that point all I could do at my current church was sit around and mourn.

Shortly thereafter I moved my membership and thus began the First Baptist of Chattanooga chapter of my life. For the longest while my designated pew seat was next to Frank and Rolena.

Rolena has taught me that friendships flourish when treated with kind words and hugs and that a happy family doesn't just fall out of the sky but is the result of a lifetime of deliberate, loving actions.

And then there was Grandma. The mark Grandma Sweat had on my life can't be denied even if a lot of it is negative. I knew when she told me to do something, I'd better do it; and the quicker I did it, the better it would be for me.

The summer Mama sent my sister and me to live at her house still lingers with me seventy years later.

As a youngster, I gathered dirt like some people gathered flowers. Grandma refused me entrance inside the house until I hosed down. My table manners would have embarrassed Emily Post. She slowed me down and insisted I eat certain foods before gorging myself on sweets.

Those back-porch talk sessions were something else. There would be five or more occupied rocking chairs. That being said, there wasn't any doubt she pulled the biggest weight. She'd rock back and forth and make comments on anything and everything.

It could be a gossip session or her take on national news. I remember she loved FDR but disliked "that negra-loving wife" of his, Eleanor. The only thing that would hush her up was stormy weather. I'm sure a lot of that stemmed from the untimely death of her son and my father. She'd herd us away to a bedroom, and we weren't allowed to talk until the storm had passed.

Grandma gave birth to four sons and three daughters and was happiest when all of them, including the in-laws, gathered for family reunions at Thanksgiving, Christmas, and summertime. I spent lots of time dodging kisses from people I wouldn't see again until the next reunion.

Her kitchen fascinated me. She had a fancy stove that was a forerunner of today's warming shelves. That's where the pies would be stashed until the big bell by the side of the well gave the signal it was time to eat.

We were part of the "children are to be seen and not heard" era, so we waited and waited while grown-ups ate their bellies full and swapped tons of stories. Grandma kept cakes in a tiny closet off the main dining area. To be summoned back there for a treat brought joy to my heart, not to mention my tummy.

By our standards, Grandma's family was rich while my family scraped the barrel to stay alive. She had her own nursery for growing plants, a washing machine, a motorized well, a forerunner of an inside waterworks, and lived in the same house all of her married life.

When one of my uncles came in his truck to take us to the Forks, Mama was still hand-scrubbing our clothes and drawing our water from a bucket. But worst of all, we were always moving.

I noted Grandma's unkind remarks about or to others. They cut like a knife. I watched as she used words to get across her feelings. She had an "I'm better than thou" air. She was large and tall and wore eyeglasses, and her white hair was wound tightly.

We children knew Grandma's parlor room was off limits—a holy family shrine. A cousin of mine who died in the Korean conflict and my brother Harold, a former Marine with a booze problem, both laid in state in the parlor room prior to their funerals.

I wish that just once she had cuddled me in her arms and told me I was a special gift from God. She never did. All I remember are her reprimands and occasionally a food treat.

Since my grandparents had given my oldest brother a home during his senior year in high school, they obviously felt that absolved them from helping the rest of us. What I've carried away from all this is a strong feeling that money and things don't equate to happiness—and a religion that hordes is alien to the gospel of Jesus Christ.

Chapter 22

Finding, Giving Grace

"It never occurred to me that God might want to change me..."

Flashbacks and reality sometimes clashed as I parented my son. For the most part those days, 1960-1985, are remembered as a wellspring of happiness. However, I was still locked in to the belief that homosexuality was a sin and that if a homosexual wanted to, he could change.

I kept praying, "Please, Father, if Alan is gay then change him." It never occurred to me that God might want to change me rather than my son.

The fact that Alan had turned his life over to Jesus when he was six encouraged me. Amid his struggles for sexual identity Alan had graduated from a church-related university, given two years of missionary service abroad, and attended seminary classes for one year.

As I reflected on Alan's personal faith journey and the integrity of his life, I wrestled with the conflict between those skimpy, yet specific, passages that seemingly abhor homosexuality and the abundant "whosoever will" verses.

Ultimately, the "whosoever will" verses won out.

When Alan disclosed to me he was gay, I had to rethink my whole theological belief system. What didn't change? Forgiveness, grace, love, and peace remained.

What moved out were my cockiness and my reliance on biblical proofs. There was no way I could win a biblical position favorable to homosexuality. That wasn't the miracle God had for me.

Instead, God removed my desire to prove anything and everything by finding verses of Scripture to buttress my view that God is an includer rather than an excluder. I could now rely on real faith. I don't have all the answers, and I never will. Instead, I'll faith it. Case dismissed.

This I know: I am at peace with my son's sexual orientation. I am at peace with myself, my son, and my Lord.

When the problem became more than I could understand and handle, I entrusted it into God's keeping and asked for the gift of peace. Today, God's peace envelopes me. It is my stay in good times and when trouble rears its head.

I will let others judge the issue as they deem best. However, I am confident that both my son and I have the loving arms of Jesus around us. With this assurance I face the future with peace, expectancy, and love.

God's peace to me was a gift, not earned or deserved. It was God's to give and mine to receive and to treasure. God's peace frees me to help others who face hurting problems.

I am sustained and propelled by Eugene Peterson's take on Jesus' words in Matthew 25:34-40 (*The Message*):

> *The king will say to those on his right, "Enter, you who are blessed by my Father! Take what's coming to you in this kingdom. It's been ready for you since the world's foundation. And here's why:*
>
> *I was hungry and you fed me,*
> *I was thirsty and you gave me a drink,*
> *I was homeless and you gave me a room,*
> *I was shivering and you gave me clothes,*
> *I was sick and you stopped to visit,*
> *I was in prison and you came to me."*
>
> *Then those "sheep" are going to say, "Master, what are you talking about? When did we ever see you hungry and feed you, thirsty and give you a drink? And when did we ever see you sick or in prison and come to you?" Then the king will say, "I'm telling the solemn truth: Whenever you did one of these things to someone overlooked or ignored, that was me—you did it to me."*

It was just after my husband's death that I knew for certain the worth of a compassionate, loving son. After he returned home to San Francisco, Alan called often and insisted that I come for a visit.

Claude died in April 1994, and by the middle of May I flew to San Francisco. We had a grand time at a rented cabin in Mendocino where we explored the area and took turns reading aloud to each other Bailey White's novel, *Mama Makes Up Her Mind*. We also took a train ride through the redwood forest.

Since that time I spend every Christmas with Alan and his partner Timothy. We have established some rituals of our own. I get a spa treatment, have English tea at the Ritz Carlton, attend a Christmas play or symphony, attend Christmas Eve services at the Episcopal Church, and help decorate their Christmas tree.

Since Alan's work is in San Francisco, New York, and London, they live in

Berkeley during the week and spend weekends at River Myst Haven in Healdsburg, California. In addition to Christmas, I visit Alan and Timothy in the spring and summer each year. Also, Alan and I usually meet in Atlanta on my birthday.

My eightieth birthday celebration, however, was held in Chattanooga so that other family members and friends could join us.

The relationship Alan and I have is far more than genetic. We are bonded by mutual love, respect, and sensitivity. Alan is my joy, my encourager, and at times my confronter.

It was never hard for me to believe or trust Alan's viewpoint, even when it radically differed from my own. Trust had been the building blocks of our relationship, even prior to his birth.

From the moment I knew I was pregnant I began to thank God for the child in my womb and to prepare myself spiritually for that grand arrival.

This is not meant to imply that I was a perfect parent or that my son always towed the line. It is meant to convey that trust, honesty, and love have and always will be the cement that binds us to each other. The passage of time makes our truth, honesty, and love grow dearer.

It seems that one day God said to me:

> *Lynelle, I'm giving you and Claude a baby boy. Model for him*
> *what it means to be a Christian. Along the way questions without*
> *answers will come your way. Remember, I had personal questions*
> *in Gethsemane and again as I hung from a Roman cross. I didn't*
> *get affirming answers either. Hold my hand, even when you can't*
> *see a step in front of you. I'll always be there for you. Keep the faith!*

Peace, like the word love, is often maligned in its usage. We are constantly invading its perimeters, changing its meaning, and diluting its influence.

The greeting, "The peace of the Lord be always with you," is part of the worship ritual of many churches. Such a greeting suggests there is something unique and enabling about the peace of the Lord.

I was seeking an inward, personal peace that would be evident to me and to others. I craved a peace that would spill over into how I lived each day. The more I sought peace, the more it eluded me.

I grappled for prayer answers through whispers and screams. I begged and demanded. I quoted Scripture and expected a miracle. Yet, I got no results, or worse, got what I didn't want.

Worry, worry, worry...I am an inveterate worrier. My friends tell me when I don't have something legitimate to worry about I'm apt to conjure up a problem. But worry contributed nothing to bringing me solutions. Worry only clouded a given issue rendering me inept to deal with it. Even worse, it negatively perpetuated the worry cycle.

It is easy to fall into the worry mode, to wring one's hands, and to weep. Meanwhile, you do nothing constructive toward eliminating your problem. Worry and faith aren't good companions. As long as I coddled my bag of worries, I sent my faith on an extended vacation.

In my eighty years of living I've spent too much time spinning my mental wheels, charged by a barrage of "what ifs." I always thought I had to have answers.

So, I went to bed with my burdens. I tossed and turned through the night hours, unable to turn loose of my heavy load. I prayed for release while holding tenaciously to my fears.

Could I really trust God? I mean, totally and completely allow God to work things out? Instead of trusting, I kept trying to put in my two cents worth. How arrogant of me to think God needed my help!

As long as I did, my burden remained. I was held hostage, not because God didn't want to free me, but because I refused his intervention.

Gradually I began to realize that Christian faith means to put all our past, present, and future in the hands of Jesus and to leave the results to him. I began to understand that faith isn't something you put in a test tube and analyze.

Slowly I began to see faith as a multifaceted experience involving complete trust, with no demands for answers or proof. For me to have faith was to trust everything to Jesus.

I can't tell you the exact time or place when I received the gift of peace. I'm sure it didn't happen in one earth-shattering experience. I think it evolved as my trust and love levels rose.

Personal peace is difficult to explain. It is something that when you have it, you know it. When it is absent, regardless of how much you fake it, you're aware of its absence.

Peace isn't a holy blotter that soaks up your pain, leaving you with a basketful of good feelings.

Peace doesn't come with a set of earmuffs that keeps you from hearing the hurts of humanity; rather it provides an amplifier for awareness.

Peace doesn't remove storms from your life; instead it gives you an anchor that enables you to withstand violent confrontations. The absence of peace is to walk around in a shroud of fear.

Peace, for me, includes being open, vulnerable, and taking risks. Every time I open up and reveal to someone that my son is gay, I feel a burst of freedom. There is something about sharing my vulnerability with others that fosters peace.

Perhaps it is the letting go of something that might bring rejection that touches others in a unique way.

God's peace is steadfast. Even when the edges unravel, peace remains constant, bringing contentment and release. I finally learned that the heavy emotional loads get less heavy when shared.

Epilogue

Alan is now in a long and committed relationship with his partner Timothy. When they exchanged civil vows in 1999, they asked me to be a part of the service and I readily agreed. This is the prayer I offered:

> *Lord Jesus,*
> *In this sacred hour I gladly commend Timothy and Alan into your gracious keeping. I thank you for their individual faith journeys. I thank you that neither of them has allowed the world at large to sully their view of a God of grace, mercy, and love. In the days that lie ahead may they individually and together draw upon and deepen their faith experiences.*
> *I ask that we, the families of Timothy and Alan, be for them an anchor when bad times come, and a gurgling mountain stream during their good times. Thank you for the friends of Alan and Timothy gathered here today. Bless each of them with a touch of your grace.*
> *O, Lord, I ask that Alan's and Timothy's love for each other, couched in their individual self-respect, flourish in the nitty-gritty acts of daily living. Remind us all that love is perishable and must be carefully tended.*
> *Father, in a world with too much hate and not enough love; too much doubt and not enough trust; too much tunnel vision and not enough faith; too much fatalism and not enough hope; too much pain and not enough joy; too much reality and not enough fantasy; too much war and not enough peace; too much work and not enough play; too many tears and not enough laughter—help us to major on the "not enoughs."*
> *Please hear this mother's prayer as we send Timothy and Alan on their way with faith, family, and friends to sustain their journey.*
> *In Jesus' name, Amen.*

Someone told me that after my prayer there wasn't a dry eye among the gathered group of well-wishers. Perhaps we all need more of the "not enoughs."

Bouquet of Thanks

The longer I live, the more I'm convinced family is one of God's most precious gifts. My sons Alan and Max, my grandson Patrick, and my great-granddaughter Ashton enrich my life daily.

My surrogate family includes the Class of 1953, University of Mary Hardin-Baylor. Like my real mom, they think I'm a lot smarter than I really am. I try to keep them thinking that way.

The early-on support given me by Dr. Paul Simmons, Phyllis Tickle, and Phyllis Edgerly Ring made me refuse to let go of my dream that my story would someday be in print.

It was Dr. John Pierce who organized my rambling stories into a readable format. Thank you, Johnny.

This book is especially dedicated to my son, Alan, who applauds all my efforts and emboldens me to think the best is yet to be.

CPSIA information can be obtained at www.ICGtesting.com
Printed in the USA
LVOW020713171112

307777LV00001B/12/P